All About

MY INVENTION

An Inventor's Planner & Journal

January – March

Andrea Hence Evans, Esq.

All About My Invention

Published by
The Law Firm of Andrea Hence Evans, LLC
Copyright© 2020
Andrea Hence Evans Esq.

ISBN: 978-1-7343298-2-7

Contact the Law Firm of Andrea Hence Evans, LLC for bulk ordering.

info@evansiplaw.com
www.evansiplaw.com
(301)497-9997
@evansiplaw

All About My Invention

An Inventors Planner & Journal

January - March

_____

(Year)

Andrea Hence Evans, Esq
The Law Firm of Andrea Hence Evans, LLC

THE LAW FIRM OF
ANDREA HENCE EVANS
PATENT · TRADEMARK · COPYRIGHT

DEDICATION

This book is dedicated to all inventors, especially my clients that trust their inventions with my Firm, The Law Firm of Andrea Hence Evans, LLC, and allow me to live my dream and be an extension of their team.

This book is dedicated to my Aunt Glorita McAfee Comacho for her continued support and encouragement.

This book is dedicated to my Aunt L. Marilyn Crawford for setting an example of a strong and successful business owner and mentor.

This book is dedicated to my father and mother-in-law, Meredith and Ellen Dean Evans, for always believing in me.

This book is dedicated to my father, Andre Hence, for his support and feedback.

This book is dedicated to my mother, Bernadette Hence, for her wisdom and confidence.

This book is dedicated to my children, Nya and Austin, who can do anything they put their minds to!

This book is dedicated to my husband, Christopher, for his unconditional love and support.

Thank you Elly Virtually, LLC for your creativity.

ALL ABOUT

MY

INVENTION

January - March

_____

(Year)

This Journal Belongs to:

_____

Address: _____

_____

_____

Phone Number: _____

Email: _____

Invest In Your Idea®

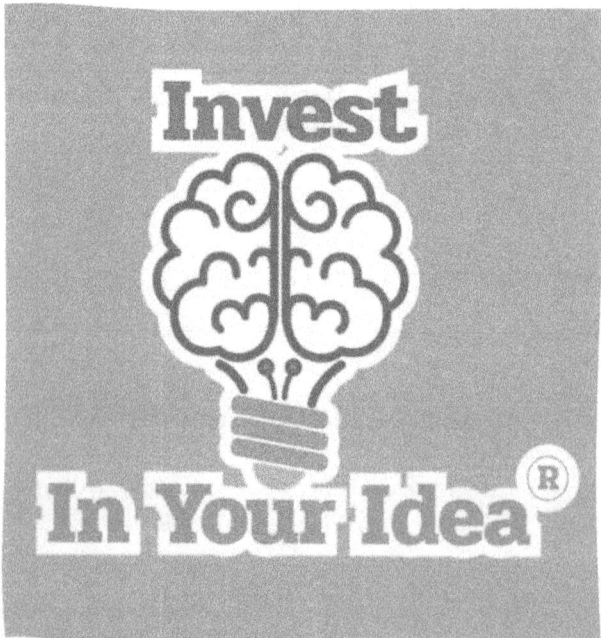

I AM AN INVENTOR!

INTRODUCTION

How exciting!

You are minding your own business and then, it hits you! Your "aha" moment. I am referring to that moment when you realize that you've come up with a better way to do something.

You have figured out a way to make it easier! You have an improvement to an existing problem, now what?

Are you ready to protect your invention?
Is all of your information about the invention in one place?
Did you document important dates?
Who did you talk to?
When did you research the invention?
What is the invention?
Why did you invent the invention?

I'm sure you have these questions and many more!

All About MY Invention: An Inventor's Planner & Journal will assist you in collecting all of your important information about your invention and help you to document it in one place.

This journal combines over a decade of educational experience, work experience, and hands-on patent examination experience to help inventors.

Enjoy

-Andrea

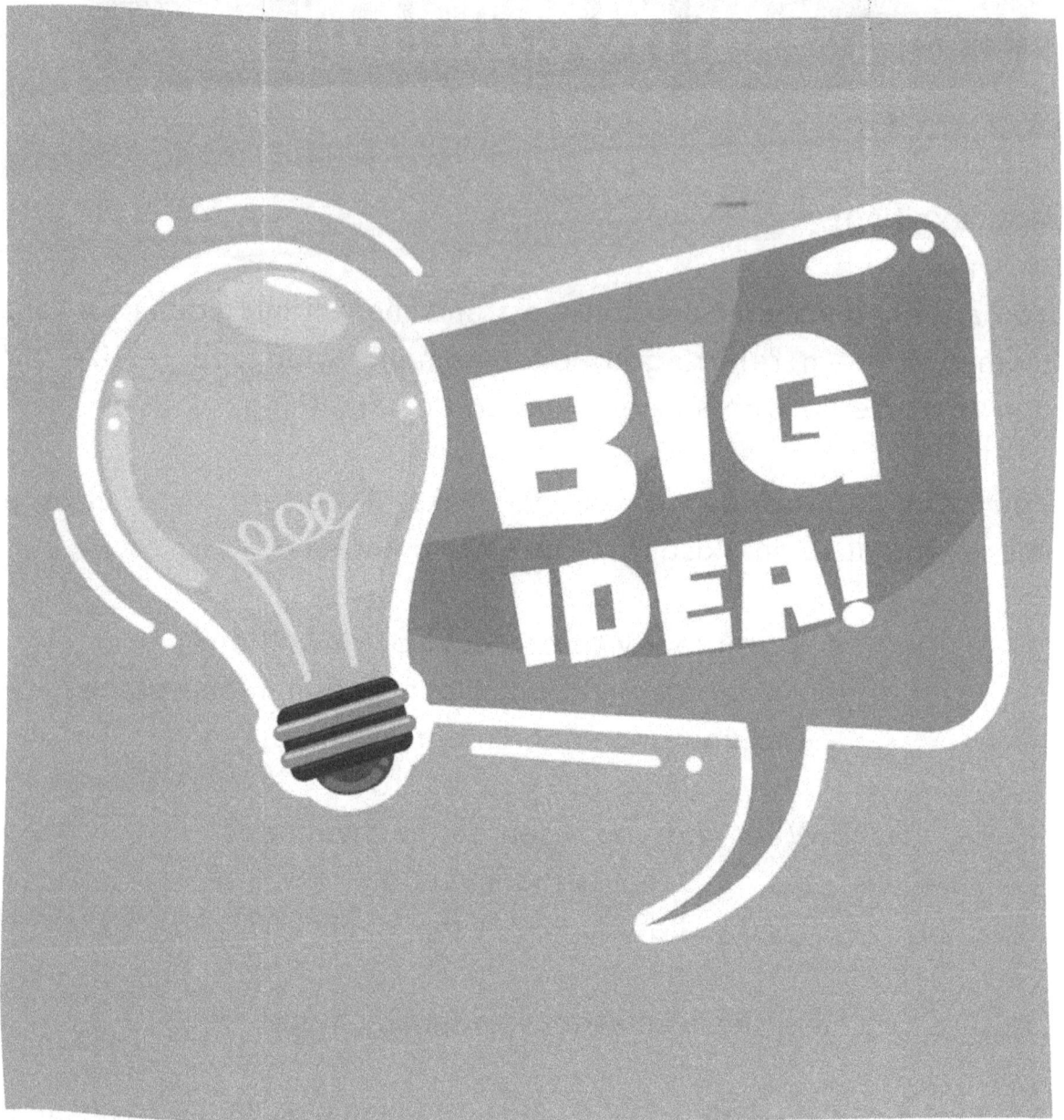

ALL ABOUT MY INVENTION

DESCRIBE YOUR INVENTION:

_____
_____
_____
_____
_____
_____
_____
_____

MY INVENTION SOLVES THESE PROBLEMS:

_____
_____
_____
_____
_____
_____
_____
_____
_____
_____
_____

ALL ABOUT MY INVENTION

MY COMPETITORS ARE:

_____

_____

_____

_____

_____

_____

_____

_____

THINGS TO DO:

- ○ _____
- ○ _____
- ○ _____
- ○ _____
- ○ _____
- ○ _____
- ○ _____
- ○ _____
- ○ _____
- ○ _____
- ○ _____

IS MY INVENTION PATENTABLE?

Here are four questions to ask to determine if your invention is patentable:

- Is it novel?

- Is it obvious?

- Was it made public more than one year prior to filing?

- Does it lack utility or usefulness?

Here's what you need to know about patentable inventions:

1. When you invent something, the invention is required to be useful and solve a problem.

2. The invention is required to be novel or new. If you notice that something already exists that's identical to what you're doing, even if that person has not filed a patent application on that invention, the invention is not patentable because the invention is not new or novel since it already exists.

3. The invention must be non-obvious. That is, would it be obvious to one of ordinary skill in the art, to take what's out there and combine it to make the invention. For example, changing the size, shape, color, material or attaching a button instead of a zipper on something are typically obvious changes such that an invention would not be patentable.

4. If an invention is made public more than one year prior to filing, then the invention is barred from being patented.

Important

MY PRIOR ART

Have you searched high and low for your invention in every store and you can't seem to find it on the shelves?

Don't assume that if you haven't seen your invention in the store, you can patent it.

Prior art is anything that exists prior to you filing a patent application.

Prior art can be a publication, patent application, patent, or even a presentation, just to name a few.

NOTES

_____

_____

_____

_____

_____

_____

_____

_____

_____

_____

_____

My Research

PATENTS OF INTEREST:

_____
_____
_____
_____

PUBLICATIONS OF INTEREST:

_____
_____
_____
_____

WEBSITES OF INTEREST:

_____
_____
_____
_____

MISCELLANEOUS INFORMATION OF INTEREST:

_____
_____
_____
_____

MY QUESTIONS

MY PATENT APPLICATION CHECKLIST

Use this section to help you to organize the details of your invention.

The specification should include a clear and concise title of the invention, background of the invention, which can provide a summary of the invention and a brief description of the drawings, a detailed description of the invention, claims, and an abstract that briefly describes the technical nature of the invention.

- [ ] Title of the Invention

- [ ] Field of the Invention – In 1-2 sentences, describe the invention.

- [ ] Background of the Invention – Describe the general background of the subject matter of the invention.

- [ ] Summary of the Invention – Provide a summary of the invention in 1-3 paragraphs.

- [ ] Brief Description of the Drawings – Describe all figures/drawings.

- [ ] Detailed Description of the Invention – Provide a detailed description of all drawings and describe all features of the invention.

- [ ] Claims- Draft claim language that identifies the patentable features of the invention. Ensure that these features are described in the detailed description section.

- [ ] Abstract of the Disclosure – Describe the patentable features of the invention.

MY PATENT APPLICATION

TITLE OF THE INVENTION:

_____

_____

_____

_____

FIELD OF THE INVENTION:

_____

_____

_____

_____

_____

BACKGROUND OF THE INVENTION:

_____

_____

_____

_____

_____

SUMMARY OF THE INVENTION:

_____

_____

_____

_____

_____

MY DRAWINGS & DESCRIPTION OF THE DRAWINGS

Figure 1

Figure 2

DETAILED DESCRIPTION OF THE INVENTION

CLAIMS

ABSTRACT

JANUARY

DREAM IT.
DO IT.

JANUARY:

SUNDAY	MONDAY	TUESDAY	WEDNESDAY

THURSDAY	FRIDAY	SATURDAY	IMPORTANT
			☐ _____
			☐ _____
			☐ _____
			☐ _____
			☐ _____
			☐ _____
			☐ _____
			☐ _____
			☐ _____
			☐ _____
			☐ _____
			☐ _____
			☐ _____

NOTES

SUNDAY:

MY INVENTION IS:

_____
_____
_____
_____

_____
_____
_____
_____
_____

DRAWINGS

I ACCOMPLISHED	DATE	THINGS TO DO
1. _____		• _____
2. _____		• _____
3. _____		• _____
4. _____		• _____
5. _____		• _____

GOALS

- ○ _____
- ○ _____
- ○ _____
- ○ _____
- ○ _____
- ○ _____

I NEED

- ☐ _____
- ☐ _____
- ☐ _____
- ☐ _____
- ☐ _____
- ☐ _____

MY NOTES

MONDAY:

MY INVENTION IS: _____

_____

_____

_____

_____

NOTES

_____

_____

_____

_____

_____

DRAWINGS

I ACCOMPLISHED	DATE	THINGS TO DO
1. _____		• _____
2. _____		• _____
3. _____		• _____
4. _____		• _____
5. _____		• _____

GOALS

- ○ _____
- ○ _____
- ○ _____
- ○ _____
- ○ _____
- ○ _____

I NEED

- ☐ _____
- ☐ _____
- ☐ _____
- ☐ _____
- ☐ _____
- ☐ _____

MY NOTES

TUESDAY:

MY INVENTION IS: _____

_____
_____
_____
_____

NOTES

_____
_____
_____
_____
_____

DRAWINGS

I ACCOMPLISHED	DATE	THINGS TO DO
1. _____		• _____
2. _____		• _____
3. _____		• _____
4. _____		• _____
5. _____		• _____

GOALS

I NEED

- ○ _____
- ○ _____
- ○ _____
- ○ _____
- ○ _____
- ○ _____

- ☐ _____
- ☐ _____
- ☐ _____
- ☐ _____
- ☐ _____
- ☐ _____

MY NOTES

WEDNESDAY:

MY INVENTION IS: _____

_____
_____
_____
_____

_____
_____
_____
_____
_____

DRAWINGS

I ACCOMPLISHED	DATE	THINGS TO DO
1. _____		• _____
2. _____		• _____
3. _____		• _____
4. _____		• _____
5. _____		• _____

GOALS

○ _____

○ _____

○ _____

○ _____

○ _____

○ _____

I NEED

☐ _____

☐ _____

☐ _____

☐ _____

☐ _____

☐ _____

MY NOTES

_____

_____

_____

_____

_____

_____

_____

_____

_____

_____

_____

_____

_____

_____

_____

_____

_____

_____

_____

_____

THURSDAY:

MY INVENTION IS: _____

_____
_____
_____
_____

_____
_____
_____
_____
_____

DRAWINGS

I ACCOMPLISHED	DATE	THINGS TO DO
1. _____		• _____
2. _____		• _____
3. _____		• _____
4. _____		• _____
5. _____		• _____

GOALS

- ○ _____
- ○ _____
- ○ _____
- ○ _____
- ○ _____
- ○ _____

I NEED

- ☐ _____
- ☐ _____
- ☐ _____
- ☐ _____
- ☐ _____
- ☐ _____

MY NOTES

FRIDAY:

MY INVENTION IS: _____
_____
_____
_____
_____

_____
_____
_____
_____
_____

DRAWINGS

I ACCOMPLISHED	DATE	THINGS TO DO
1. _____		• _____
2. _____		• _____
3. _____		• _____
4. _____		• _____
5. _____		• _____

GOALS

I NEED

- ○ _____
- ○ _____
- ○ _____
- ○ _____
- ○ _____
- ○ _____

- ☐ _____
- ☐ _____
- ☐ _____
- ☐ _____
- ☐ _____
- ☐ _____

MY NOTES

SATURDAY:

MY INVENTION IS: _____
_____
_____
_____
_____

NOTES
_____
_____
_____
_____
_____

DRAWINGS

I ACCOMPLISHED	DATE	THINGS TO DO
1. _____		• _____
2. _____		• _____
3. _____		• _____
4. _____		• _____
5. _____		• _____

GOALS

- ○ _____
- ○ _____
- ○ _____
- ○ _____
- ○ _____
- ○ _____

I NEED

- ☐ _____
- ☐ _____
- ☐ _____
- ☐ _____
- ☐ _____
- ☐ _____

MY NOTES

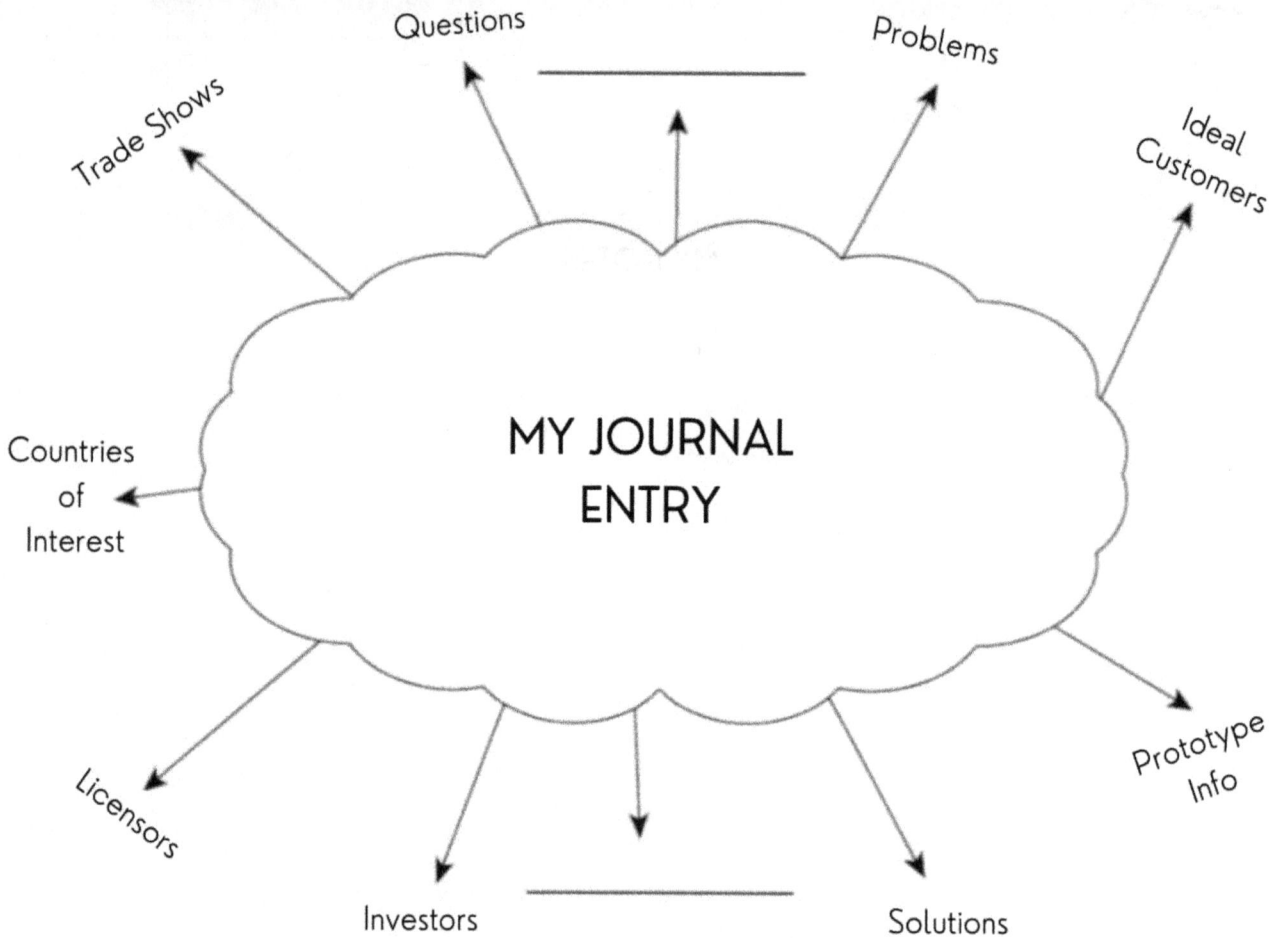

Questions

Problems

Trade Shows

Ideal Customers

Countries of Interest

MY JOURNAL ENTRY

Licensors

Investors

Solutions

Prototype Info

MY JOURNAL ENTRY FOR THE WEEK OF:

MY JOURNAL ENTRY FOR THE WEEK OF:

RESOURCES

_____
_____
_____
_____
_____
_____
_____

REFERENCES

_____
_____
_____
_____
_____
_____

IMPORTANT INFORMATION ABOUT MY INVENTION

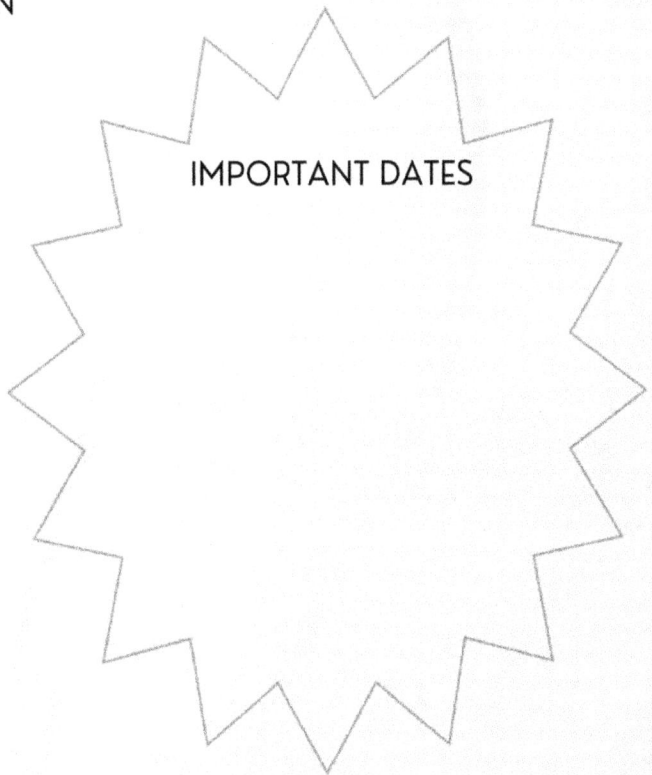

_____
_____
_____
_____
_____
_____
_____
_____
_____
_____
_____
_____

IMPORTANT DATES

I SPOKE TO

- _____
- _____
- _____
- _____
- _____
- _____

MISC.

I FEEL

happy   sad

worried   angry

SUNDAY:

MY INVENTION IS: _____

_____

_____

_____

_____

_____

_____

_____

_____

DRAWINGS

I ACCOMPLISHED	DATE	THINGS TO DO
1. _____		• _____
2. _____		• _____
3. _____		• _____
4. _____		• _____
5. _____		• _____

GOALS

- _____
- _____
- _____
- _____
- _____
- _____

I NEED

- [ ] _____
- [ ] _____
- [ ] _____
- [ ] _____
- [ ] _____
- [ ] _____

MY NOTES

MONDAY:

MY INVENTION IS: _____

_____
_____
_____
_____

NOTES

_____
_____
_____
_____
_____

DRAWINGS

I ACCOMPLISHED	DATE	THINGS TO DO
1. _____		• _____
2. _____		• _____
3. _____		• _____
4. _____		• _____
5. _____		• _____

GOALS

- ○ _____
- ○ _____
- ○ _____
- ○ _____
- ○ _____
- ○ _____

I NEED

- ☐ _____
- ☐ _____
- ☐ _____
- ☐ _____
- ☐ _____
- ☐ _____

MY NOTES

TUESDAY:

MY INVENTION IS: _____

_____

_____

_____

_____

NOTES

_____

_____

_____

_____

_____

DRAWINGS

I ACCOMPLISHED	DATE	THINGS TO DO
1. _____		• _____
2. _____		• _____
3. _____		• _____
4. _____		• _____
5. _____		• _____

GOALS

-
-
-
-
-
-

I NEED

- [ ]
- [ ]
- [ ]
- [ ]
- [ ]
- [ ]

MY NOTES

WEDNESDAY:

MY INVENTION IS:

_____

_____

_____

_____

_____

_____

_____

_____

DRAWINGS

I ACCOMPLISHED	DATE	THINGS TO DO
1. _____		• _____
2. _____		• _____
3. _____		• _____
4. _____		• _____
5. _____		• _____

GOALS

○ _____

○ _____

○ _____

○ _____

○ _____

○ _____

I NEED

☐ _____

☐ _____

☐ _____

☐ _____

☐ _____

☐ _____

MY NOTES

THURSDAY:

MY INVENTION IS: _____

_____

_____

_____

_____

NOTES

_____

_____

_____

_____

_____

DRAWINGS

I ACCOMPLISHED	DATE	THINGS TO DO
1. _____		• _____
2. _____		• _____
3. _____		• _____
4. _____		• _____
5. _____		• _____

GOALS

I NEED

MY NOTES

FRIDAY:

MY INVENTION IS: _____

_____

_____

_____

NOTES

_____

_____

_____

_____

DRAWINGS

I ACCOMPLISHED	DATE	THINGS TO DO
1. _____		• _____
2. _____		• _____
3. _____		• _____
4. _____		• _____
5. _____		• _____

GOALS

- ○ _____
- ○ _____
- ○ _____
- ○ _____
- ○ _____
- ○ _____

I NEED

- ☐ _____
- ☐ _____
- ☐ _____
- ☐ _____
- ☐ _____
- ☐ _____

MY NOTES

SATURDAY:

MY INVENTION IS: _____

_____
_____
_____
_____

_____
_____
_____
_____
_____

DRAWINGS

I ACCOMPLISHED	DATE	THINGS TO DO
1. _____		• _____
2. _____		• _____
3. _____		• _____
4. _____		• _____
5. _____		• _____

GOALS

- ○ _____
- ○ _____
- ○ _____
- ○ _____
- ○ _____
- ○ _____

I NEED

- ☐ _____
- ☐ _____
- ☐ _____
- ☐ _____
- ☐ _____
- ☐ _____

MY NOTES

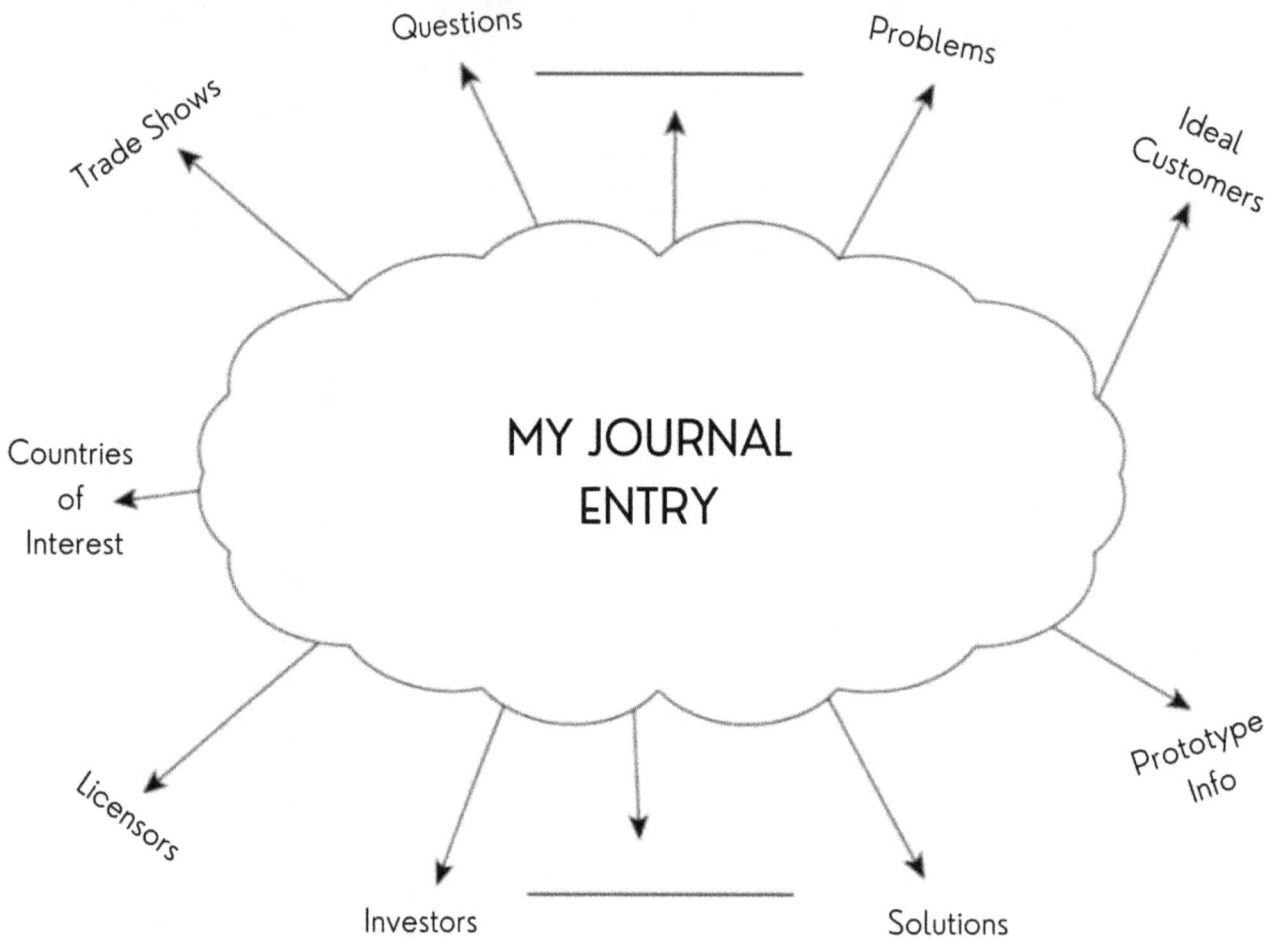

Questions

Problems

Trade Shows

Ideal Customers

Countries of Interest

MY JOURNAL ENTRY

Licensors

Investors

Solutions

Prototype Info

MY JOURNAL ENTRY FOR THE WEEK OF:

_____

_____

_____

_____

_____

_____

_____

_____

_____

_____

_____

_____

_____

_____

_____

_____

_____

_____

_____

MY JOURNAL ENTRY FOR THE WEEK OF:

RESOURCES

REFERENCES

IMPORTANT INFORMATION ABOUT MY INVENTION

IMPORTANT DATES

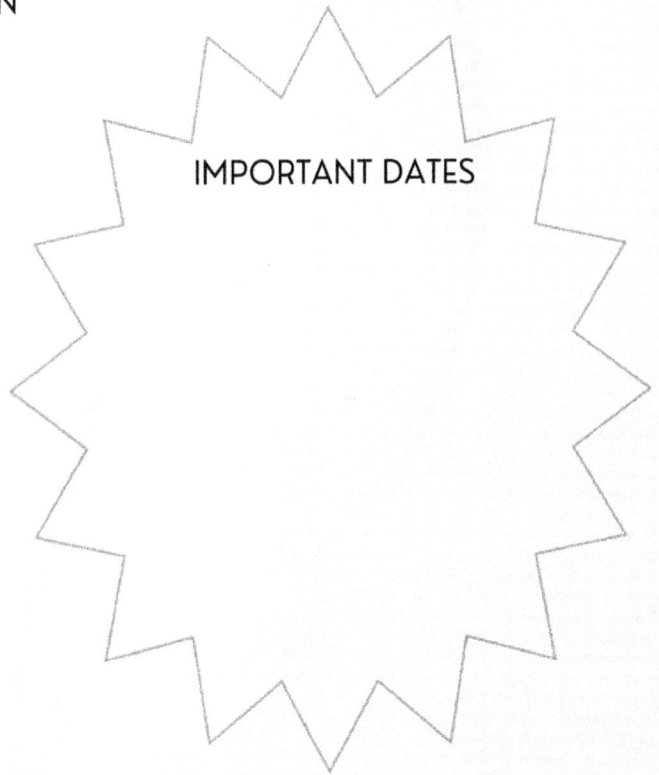

I SPOKE TO

-
-
-
-
-
-

MISC.

I FEEL

happy

sad

worried

angry

SUNDAY:

MY INVENTION IS:

_____

_____

_____

_____

NOTES

_____

_____

_____

_____

DRAWINGS

I ACCOMPLISHED	DATE	THINGS TO DO
1. _____		• _____
2. _____		• _____
3. _____		• _____
4. _____		• _____
5. _____		• _____

GOALS

- ○ _____
- ○ _____
- ○ _____
- ○ _____
- ○ _____
- ○ _____

I NEED

- ☐ _____
- ☐ _____
- ☐ _____
- ☐ _____
- ☐ _____
- ☐ _____

MY NOTES

MONDAY:

MY INVENTION IS: _____

_____
_____
_____
_____

NOTES

_____
_____
_____
_____
_____

DRAWINGS

I ACCOMPLISHED	DATE	THINGS TO DO
1. _____		• _____
2. _____		• _____
3. _____		• _____
4. _____		• _____
5. _____		• _____

GOALS

- ○ _____
- ○ _____
- ○ _____
- ○ _____
- ○ _____
- ○ _____

I NEED

- ☐ _____
- ☐ _____
- ☐ _____
- ☐ _____
- ☐ _____
- ☐ _____

MY NOTES

TUESDAY:

MY INVENTION IS: _____

_____

_____

_____

_____

_____

_____

_____

_____

_____

DRAWINGS

I ACCOMPLISHED	DATE	THINGS TO DO
1. _____		• _____
2. _____		• _____
3. _____		• _____
4. _____		• _____
5. _____		• _____

GOALS

- ○ _____
- ○ _____
- ○ _____
- ○ _____
- ○ _____
- ○ _____

I NEED

- ☐ _____
- ☐ _____
- ☐ _____
- ☐ _____
- ☐ _____
- ☐ _____

MY NOTES

WEDNESDAY:

MY INVENTION IS: _____

_____
_____
_____
_____

_____
_____
_____
_____
_____

DRAWINGS

I ACCOMPLISHED	DATE	THINGS TO DO
1. _____		• _____
2. _____		• _____
3. _____		• _____
4. _____		• _____
5. _____		• _____

GOALS

- _____
- _____
- _____
- _____
- _____
- _____

I NEED

- [ ] _____
- [ ] _____
- [ ] _____
- [ ] _____
- [ ] _____
- [ ] _____

MY NOTES

THURSDAY:

MY INVENTION IS: _____

_____

_____

_____

_____

_____

_____

_____

_____

DRAWINGS

I ACCOMPLISHED	DATE	THINGS TO DO
1. _____		• _____
2. _____		• _____
3. _____		• _____
4. _____		• _____
5. _____		• _____

GOALS	I NEED

GOALS
- ○ _____
- ○ _____
- ○ _____
- ○ _____
- ○ _____
- ○ _____

I NEED
- ☐ _____
- ☐ _____
- ☐ _____
- ☐ _____
- ☐ _____
- ☐ _____

MY NOTES

FRIDAY:

MY INVENTION IS: _____
_____
_____
_____
_____

NOTES
_____
_____
_____
_____
_____

DRAWINGS

I ACCOMPLISHED	DATE	THINGS TO DO
1. _____		• _____
2. _____		• _____
3. _____		• _____
4. _____		• _____
5. _____		• _____

GOALS

- ○ _____
- ○ _____
- ○ _____
- ○ _____
- ○ _____
- ○ _____

I NEED

- ☐ _____
- ☐ _____
- ☐ _____
- ☐ _____
- ☐ _____
- ☐ _____

MY NOTES

SATURDAY:

MY INVENTION IS: _____

_____
_____
_____
_____

_____
_____
_____
_____

DRAWINGS

I ACCOMPLISHED	DATE	THINGS TO DO
1. _____		• _____
2. _____		• _____
3. _____		• _____
4. _____		• _____
5. _____		• _____

GOALS

- ○ _____
- ○ _____
- ○ _____
- ○ _____
- ○ _____
- ○ _____

I NEED

- ☐ _____
- ☐ _____
- ☐ _____
- ☐ _____
- ☐ _____
- ☐ _____

MY NOTES

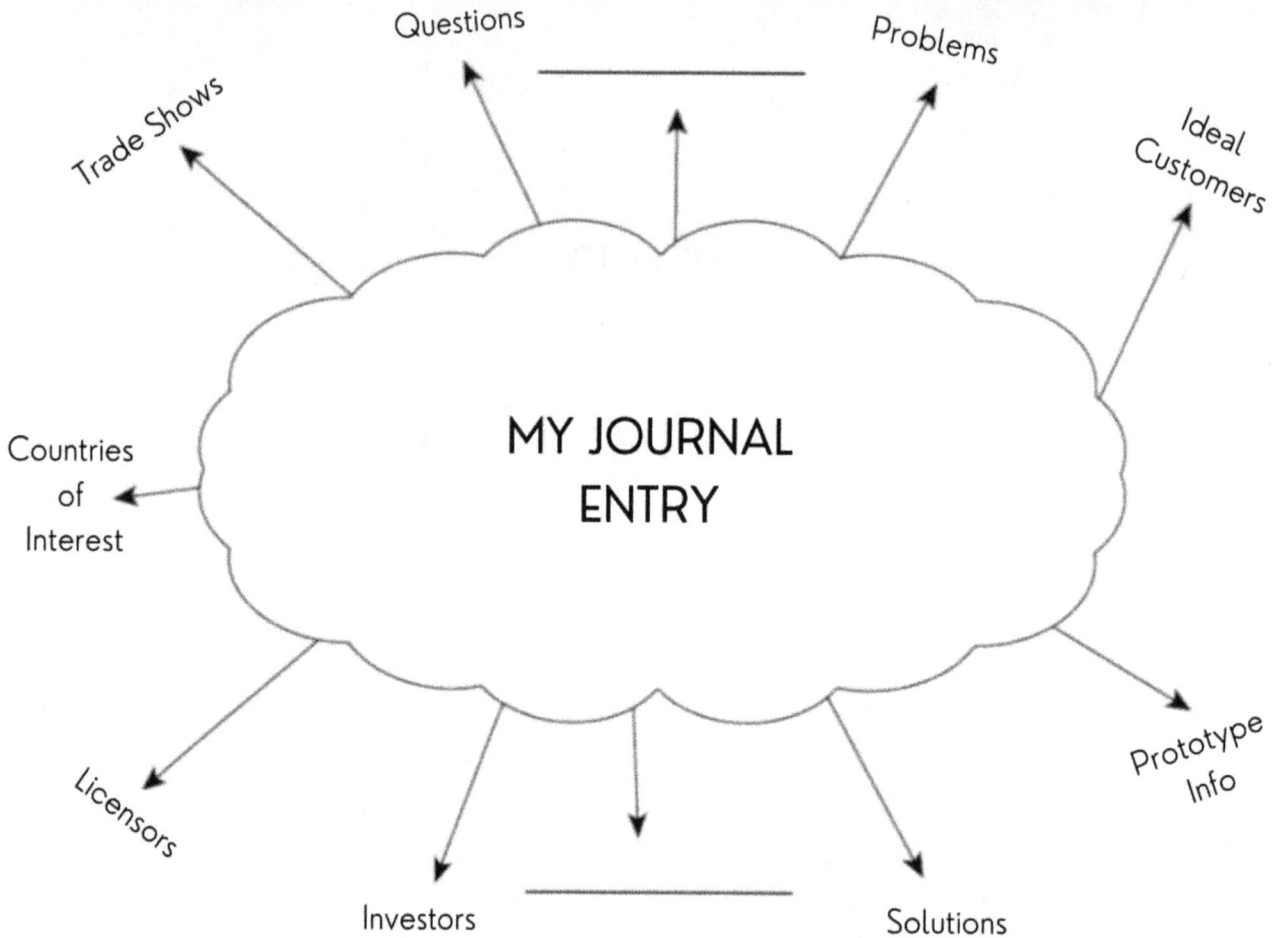

Questions

Problems

Trade Shows

Ideal Customers

MY JOURNAL ENTRY

Countries of Interest

Licensors

Investors

Solutions

Prototype Info

MY JOURNAL ENTRY FOR THE WEEK OF:

_____

_____

_____

_____

_____

_____

_____

_____

_____

_____

_____

_____

_____

_____

_____

_____

MY JOURNAL ENTRY FOR THE WEEK OF:

RESOURCES

REFERENCES

IMPORTANT INFORMATION ABOUT MY INVENTION

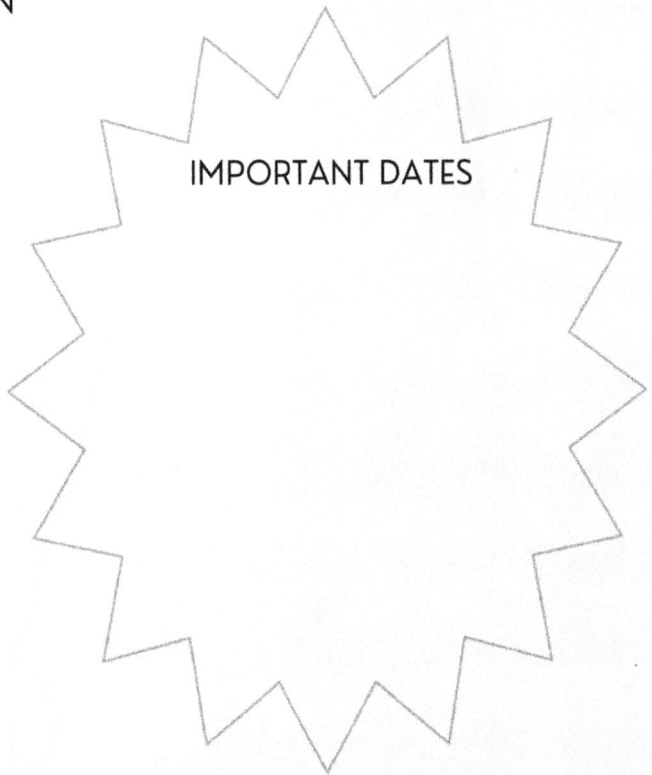

IMPORTANT DATES

I SPOKE TO

MISC.

I FEEL

happy

sad

worried

angry

SUNDAY:

MY INVENTION IS: _____
_____
_____
_____
_____

NOTES
_____
_____
_____
_____
_____

DRAWINGS

I ACCOMPLISHED	DATE	THINGS TO DO
1. _____		• _____
2. _____		• _____
3. _____		• _____
4. _____		• _____
5. _____		• _____

GOALS

- ○ _____
- ○ _____
- ○ _____
- ○ _____
- ○ _____
- ○ _____

I NEED

- ☐ _____
- ☐ _____
- ☐ _____
- ☐ _____
- ☐ _____
- ☐ _____

MY NOTES

MONDAY:

MY INVENTION IS: _____

_____
_____
_____
_____

NOTES

_____
_____
_____
_____
_____

DRAWINGS

I ACCOMPLISHED

1. _____
2. _____
3. _____
4. _____
5. _____

DATE

THINGS TO DO

- _____
- _____
- _____
- _____
- _____

GOALS

○ _____

○ _____

○ _____

○ _____

○ _____

○ _____

I NEED

☐ _____

☐ _____

☐ _____

☐ _____

☐ _____

☐ _____

MY NOTES

_____
_____
_____
_____
_____
_____
_____
_____
_____
_____
_____
_____
_____
_____
_____
_____
_____
_____
_____
_____

TUESDAY:

MY INVENTION IS: _____
_____
_____
_____
_____

NOTES
_____
_____
_____
_____
_____

DRAWINGS

I ACCOMPLISHED	DATE	THINGS TO DO
1. _____		• _____
2. _____		• _____
3. _____		• _____
4. _____		• _____
5. _____		• _____

GOALS

- _____
- _____
- _____
- _____
- _____
- _____

I NEED

- [ ] _____
- [ ] _____
- [ ] _____
- [ ] _____
- [ ] _____
- [ ] _____

MY NOTES

WEDNESDAY:

MY INVENTION IS: _____

_____

_____

_____

_____

NOTES

_____

_____

_____

_____

_____

DRAWINGS

I ACCOMPLISHED	DATE	THINGS TO DO
1. _____		• _____
2. _____		• _____
3. _____		• _____
4. _____		• _____
5. _____		• _____

GOALS

- ○ _____
- ○ _____
- ○ _____
- ○ _____
- ○ _____
- ○ _____

I NEED

- ☐ _____
- ☐ _____
- ☐ _____
- ☐ _____
- ☐ _____
- ☐ _____

MY NOTES

THURSDAY:

MY INVENTION IS: _____

_____

_____

_____

_____

NOTES

_____

_____

_____

_____

_____

DRAWINGS

I ACCOMPLISHED	DATE	THINGS TO DO
1. _____		• _____
2. _____		• _____
3. _____		• _____
4. _____		• _____
5. _____		• _____

GOALS

- ○
- ○
- ○
- ○
- ○
- ○

I NEED

- ☐
- ☐
- ☐
- ☐
- ☐
- ☐

MY NOTES

FRIDAY:

MY INVENTION IS: _____

_____

_____

_____

_____

NOTES

_____

_____

_____

_____

_____

DRAWINGS

I ACCOMPLISHED	DATE	THINGS TO DO
1. _____		• _____
2. _____		• _____
3. _____		• _____
4. _____		• _____
5. _____		• _____

GOALS

- _____
- _____
- _____
- _____
- _____
- _____

I NEED

- [ ] _____
- [ ] _____
- [ ] _____
- [ ] _____
- [ ] _____
- [ ] _____

MY NOTES

_____
_____
_____
_____
_____
_____
_____
_____
_____
_____
_____
_____
_____
_____
_____
_____
_____
_____
_____
_____
_____

SATURDAY:

MY INVENTION IS: _____

_____

_____

_____

_____

_____

_____

_____

_____

_____

DRAWINGS

I ACCOMPLISHED	DATE	THINGS TO DO
1. _____		• _____
2. _____		• _____
3. _____		• _____
4. _____		• _____
5. _____		• _____

GOALS

○ _____

○ _____

○ _____

○ _____

○ _____

○ _____

I NEED

☐ _____

☐ _____

☐ _____

☐ _____

☐ _____

☐ _____

MY NOTES

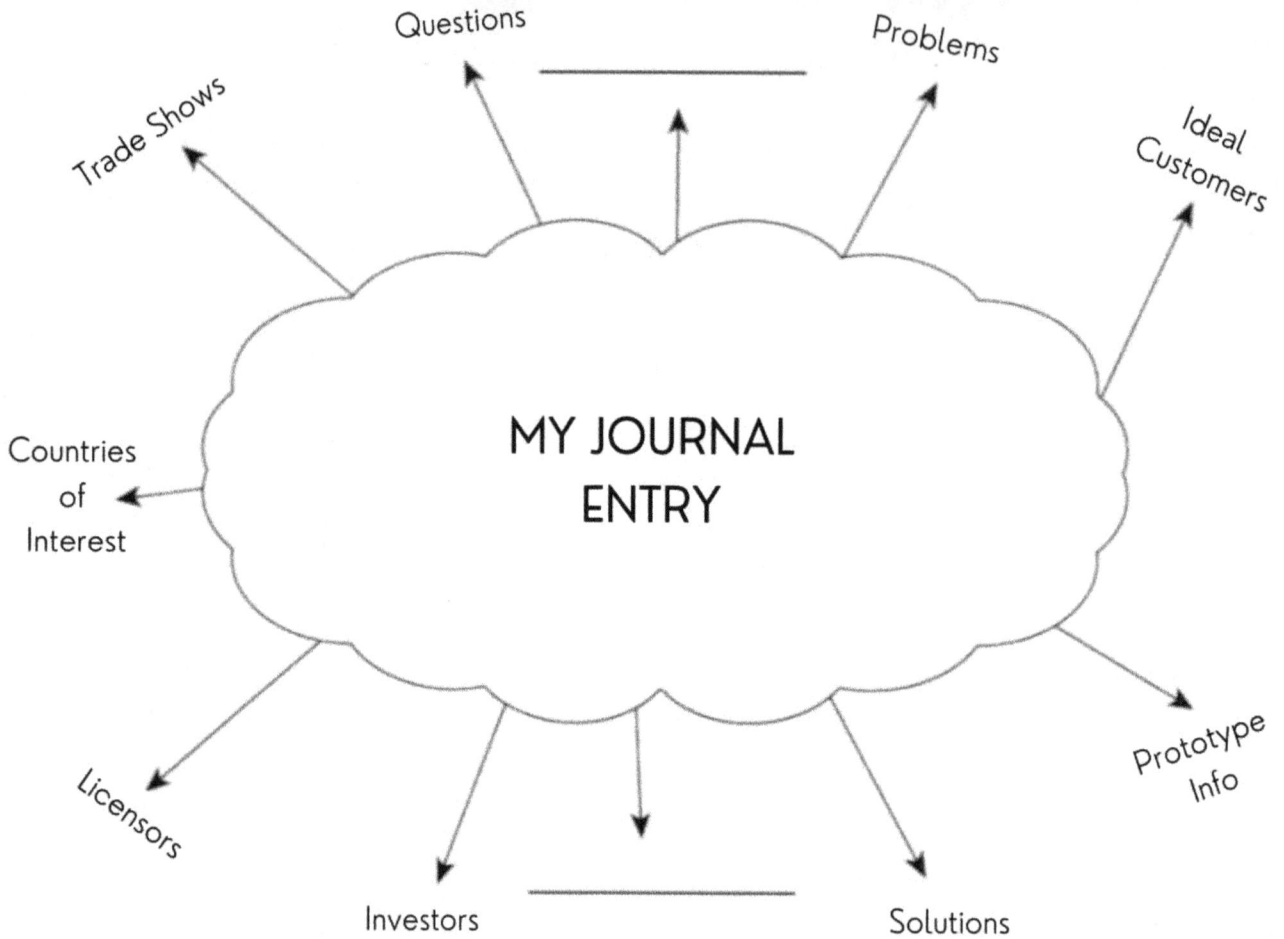

Questions

_____

Problems

Trade Shows

Ideal Customers

Countries of Interest

MY JOURNAL ENTRY

Licensors

Investors

_____

Solutions

Prototype Info

_____

_____

_____

_____

_____

_____

_____

_____

MY JOURNAL ENTRY FOR THE WEEK OF:

MY JOURNAL ENTRY FOR THE WEEK OF:

RESOURCES

REFERENCES

IMPORTANT INFORMATION ABOUT MY INVENTION

IMPORTANT DATES

I SPOKE TO

-
-
-
-
-
-

MISC.

I FEEL

happy

sad

worried

angry

I love it!

Yes!

FEBURARY

ACT ON YOUR IDEAS!

SUNDAY	MONDAY	TUESDAY	WEDNESDAY

THURSDAY	FRIDAY	SATURDAY	IMPORTANT

NOTES

MY INVENTION IS: _____

_____

_____

_____

_____

NOTES

_____

_____

_____

_____

_____

DRAWINGS

I ACCOMPLISHED	DATE	THINGS TO DO
1. _____		• _____
2. _____		• _____
3. _____		• _____
4. _____		• _____
5. _____		• _____

GOALS

- ○ _____
- ○ _____
- ○ _____
- ○ _____
- ○ _____
- ○ _____

I NEED

- ☐ _____
- ☐ _____
- ☐ _____
- ☐ _____
- ☐ _____
- ☐ _____

MY NOTES

MONDAY:

MY INVENTION IS:

_____ _____

_____

_____

_____

_____

NOTES

_____

_____

_____

_____

_____

DRAWINGS

I ACCOMPLISHED	DATE	THINGS TO DO
1. _____		• _____
2. _____		• _____
3. _____		• _____
4. _____		• _____
5. _____		• _____

GOALS

- ○ _____
- ○ _____
- ○ _____
- ○ _____
- ○ _____
- ○ _____

I NEED

- ☐ _____
- ☐ _____
- ☐ _____
- ☐ _____
- ☐ _____
- ☐ _____

MY NOTES

TUESDAY:

MY INVENTION IS: _____
_____
_____
_____
_____

NOTES
_____
_____
_____
_____
_____

DRAWINGS

I ACCOMPLISHED	DATE	THINGS TO DO
1. _____		• _____
2. _____		• _____
3. _____		• _____
4. _____		• _____
5. _____		• _____

GOALS

○ _____

○ _____

○ _____

○ _____

○ _____

○ _____

I NEED

☐ _____

☐ _____

☐ _____

☐ _____

☐ _____

☐ _____

MY NOTES

_____

_____

_____

_____

_____

_____

_____

_____

_____

_____

_____

_____

_____

_____

_____

_____

_____

_____

WEDNESDAY:

MY INVENTION IS: _____

_____

_____

_____

_____

NOTES

_____

_____

_____

_____

_____

DRAWINGS

I ACCOMPLISHED	DATE	THINGS TO DO
1. _____		• _____
2. _____		• _____
3. _____		• _____
4. _____		• _____
5. _____		• _____

GOALS

- ○ _____
- ○ _____
- ○ _____
- ○ _____
- ○ _____
- ○ _____

I NEED

- ☐ _____
- ☐ _____
- ☐ _____
- ☐ _____
- ☐ _____
- ☐ _____

MY NOTES

THURSDAY:

MY INVENTION IS: _____

_____

_____

_____

_____

_____

_____

_____

_____

_____

DRAWINGS

I ACCOMPLISHED	DATE	THINGS TO DO
1. _____		• _____
2. _____		• _____
3. _____		• _____
4. _____		• _____
5. _____		• _____

GOALS

- ○ _____
- ○ _____
- ○ _____
- ○ _____
- ○ _____
- ○ _____

I NEED

- ☐ _____
- ☐ _____
- ☐ _____
- ☐ _____
- ☐ _____
- ☐ _____

MY NOTES

FRIDAY:

MY INVENTION IS: _____

_____

_____

_____

NOTES

_____

_____

_____

_____

DRAWINGS

I ACCOMPLISHED	DATE	THINGS TO DO
1. _____		• _____
2. _____		• _____
3. _____		• _____
4. _____		• _____
5. _____		• _____

GOALS

- ○ _____
- ○ _____
- ○ _____
- ○ _____
- ○ _____
- ○ _____

I NEED

- ☐ _____
- ☐ _____
- ☐ _____
- ☐ _____
- ☐ _____
- ☐ _____

MY NOTES

SATURDAY:

MY INVENTION IS: _____
_____
_____
_____
_____

_____
_____
_____
_____
_____

DRAWINGS

I ACCOMPLISHED	DATE	THINGS TO DO
1. _____		• _____
2. _____		• _____
3. _____		• _____
4. _____		• _____
5. _____		• _____

GOALS

I NEED

MY NOTES

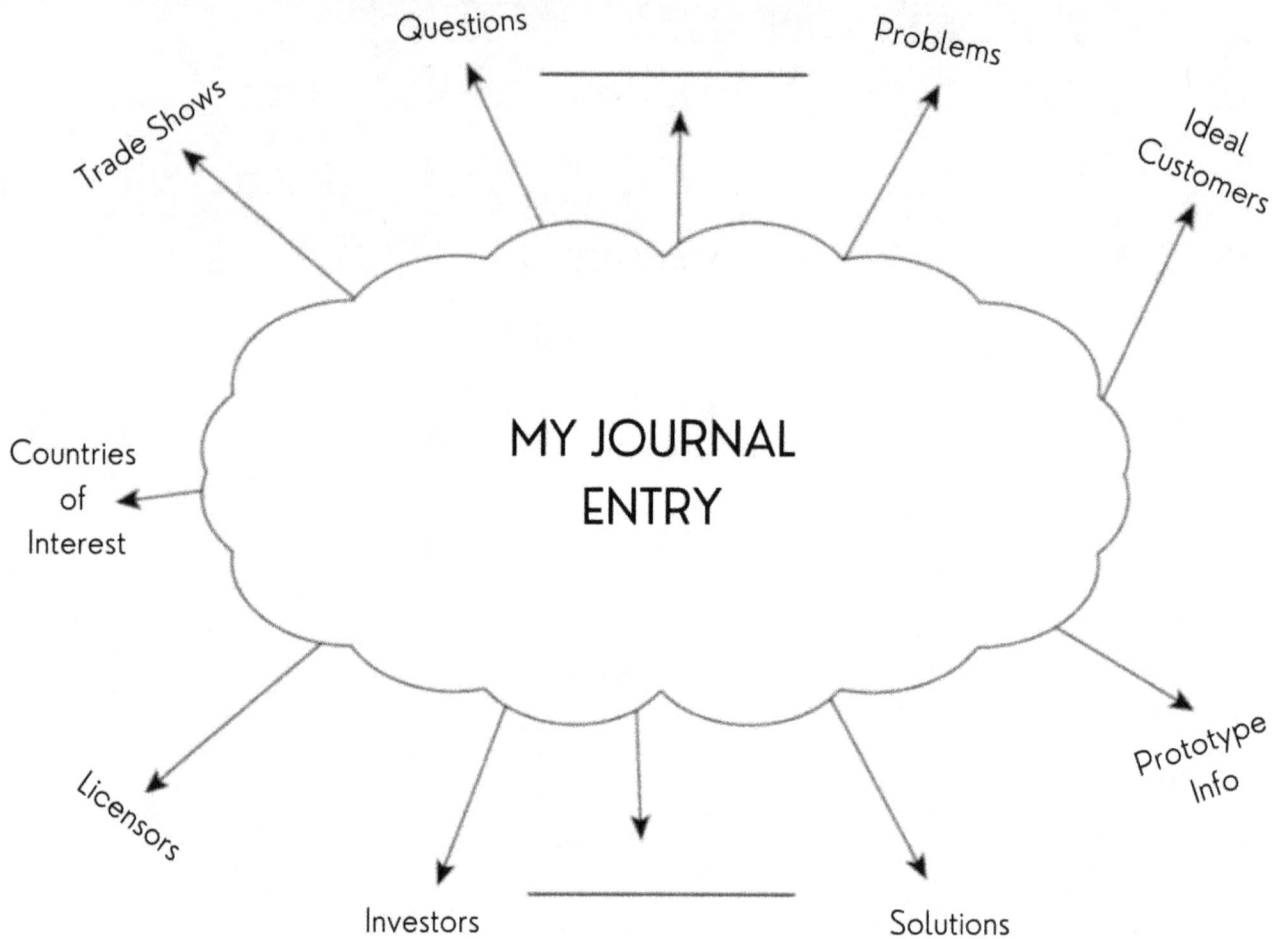

Questions

Problems

Trade Shows

Ideal Customers

Countries of Interest

MY JOURNAL ENTRY

Licensors

Prototype Info

Investors

Solutions

MY JOURNAL ENTRY FOR THE WEEK OF:

_____

_____

_____

_____

_____

_____

_____

_____

_____

_____

_____

_____

_____

_____

_____

_____

_____

MY JOURNAL ENTRY FOR THE WEEK OF:

RESOURCES	REFERENCES

IMPORTANT INFORMATION ABOUT MY INVENTION

IMPORTANT DATES

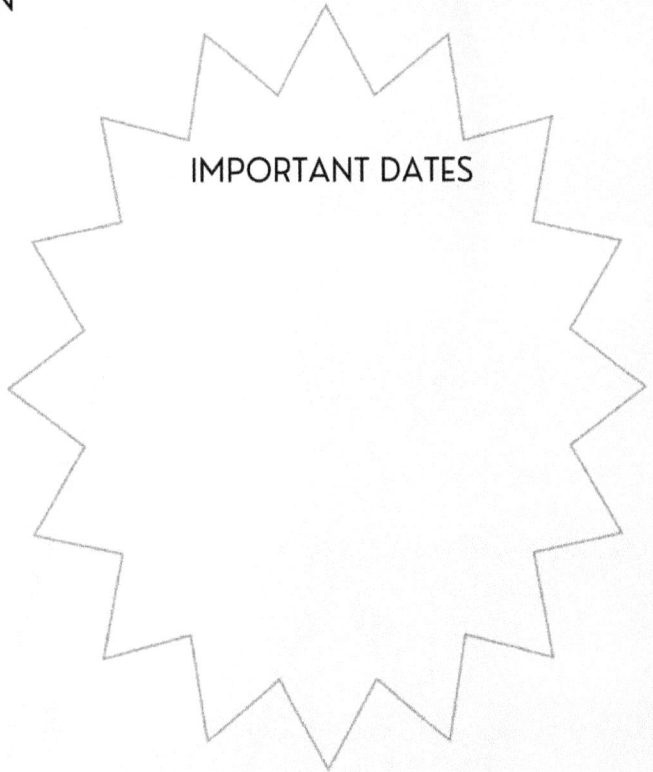

I SPOKE TO	MISC.	I FEEL
•		happy sad
•		
•		
•		worried angry
•		
•		

SUNDAY:

MY INVENTION IS: _____
_____
_____
_____
_____

NOTES
_____
_____
_____
_____
_____

DRAWINGS

I ACCOMPLISHED	DATE	THINGS TO DO
1. _____		• _____
2. _____		• _____
3. _____		• _____
4. _____		• _____
5. _____		• _____

GOALS

- ○ _____
- ○ _____
- ○ _____
- ○ _____
- ○ _____
- ○ _____

I NEED

- ☐ _____
- ☐ _____
- ☐ _____
- ☐ _____
- ☐ _____
- ☐ _____

MY NOTES

MONDAY:

MY INVENTION IS: _____

_____

_____

_____

_____

_____

_____

_____

_____

_____

DRAWINGS

I ACCOMPLISHED	DATE	THINGS TO DO
1. _____		• _____
2. _____		• _____
3. _____		• _____
4. _____		• _____
5. _____		• _____

118

GOALS

- ○ _____
- ○ _____
- ○ _____
- ○ _____
- ○ _____
- ○ _____

I NEED

- ☐ _____
- ☐ _____
- ☐ _____
- ☐ _____
- ☐ _____
- ☐ _____

MY NOTES

TUESDAY:

MY INVENTION IS: _____

_____

_____

_____

_____

_____

_____

_____

_____

_____

DRAWINGS

I ACCOMPLISHED	DATE	THINGS TO DO
1. _____		• _____
2. _____		• _____
3. _____		• _____
4. _____		• _____
5. _____		• _____

GOALS

-
-
-
-
-
-

I NEED

- [ ]
- [ ]
- [ ]
- [ ]
- [ ]
- [ ]

MY NOTES

WEDNESDAY:

MY INVENTION IS: _____

_____
_____
_____
_____

_____
_____
_____
_____
_____

DRAWINGS

I ACCOMPLISHED	DATE	THINGS TO DO
1. _____		• _____
2. _____		• _____
3. _____		• _____
4. _____		• _____
5. _____		• _____

GOALS

- _____
- _____
- _____
- _____
- _____
- _____

I NEED

- [ ] _____
- [ ] _____
- [ ] _____
- [ ] _____
- [ ] _____
- [ ] _____

MY NOTES

THURSDAY:

MY INVENTION IS: _____
_____

_____

_____

_____

_____

_____

_____

_____

_____

DRAWINGS

I ACCOMPLISHED	DATE	THINGS TO DO
1. _____		• _____
2. _____		• _____
3. _____		• _____
4. _____		• _____
5. _____		• _____

GOALS

- ○ _____
- ○ _____
- ○ _____
- ○ _____
- ○ _____
- ○ _____

I NEED

- ☐ _____
- ☐ _____
- ☐ _____
- ☐ _____
- ☐ _____
- ☐ _____

MY NOTES

FRIDAY:

MY INVENTION IS: _____

_____
_____
_____
_____

NOTES

_____
_____
_____
_____
_____

DRAWINGS

I ACCOMPLISHED	DATE	THINGS TO DO
1. _____		• _____
2. _____		• _____
3. _____		• _____
4. _____		• _____
5. _____		• _____

GOALS	I NEED

GOALS

○ _____

○ _____

○ _____

○ _____

○ _____

○ _____

I NEED

☐ _____

☐ _____

☐ _____

☐ _____

☐ _____

☐ _____

MY NOTES

SATURDAY:

MY INVENTION IS: _____
_____
_____
_____
_____

_____
_____
_____
_____
_____

DRAWINGS

I ACCOMPLISHED	DATE	THINGS TO DO
1. _____		• _____
2. _____		• _____
3. _____		• _____
4. _____		• _____
5. _____		• _____

GOALS

- ○ _____
- ○ _____
- ○ _____
- ○ _____
- ○ _____
- ○ _____

I NEED

- ☐ _____
- ☐ _____
- ☐ _____
- ☐ _____
- ☐ _____
- ☐ _____

MY NOTES

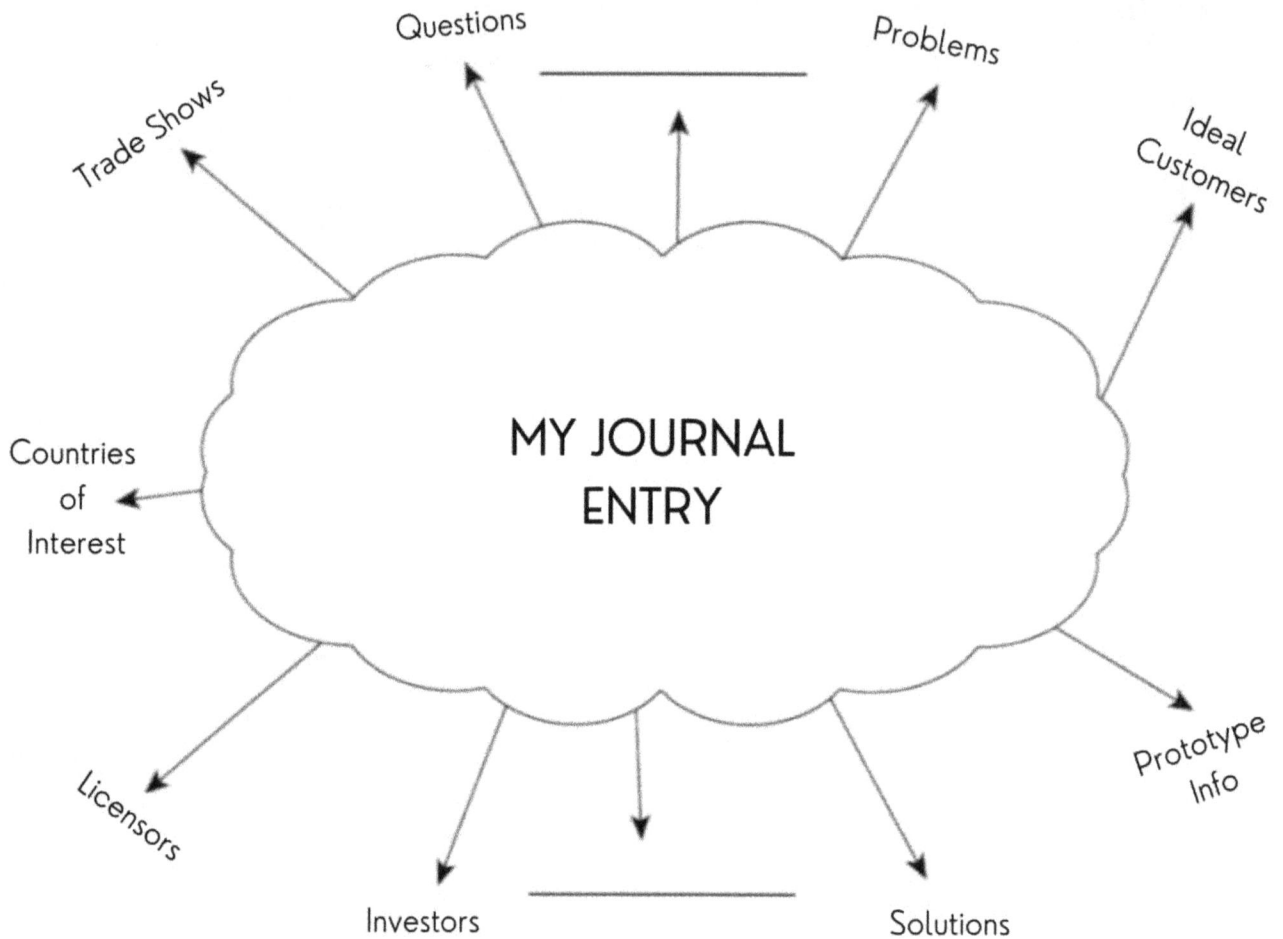

Questions _____

Problems

Trade Shows

Ideal Customers

Countries of Interest

MY JOURNAL ENTRY

Licensors

Prototype Info

Investors _____

Solutions

_____

_____

_____

_____

_____

_____

_____

MY JOURNAL ENTRY FOR THE WEEK OF:

_____

_____

_____

_____

_____

_____

_____

_____

_____

_____

_____

_____

_____

_____

_____

_____

MY JOURNAL ENTRY FOR THE WEEK OF:

RESOURCES	REFERENCES

IMPORTANT INFORMATION ABOUT MY INVENTION

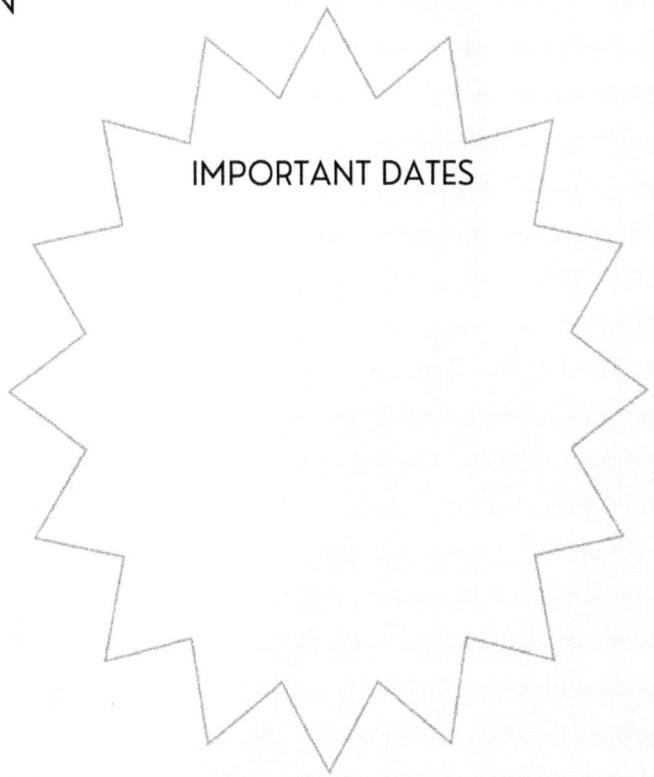

IMPORTANT DATES

I SPOKE TO	MISC.	I FEEL
•		happy sad
•		worried angry

SUNDAY:

MY INVENTION IS: _____

_____

_____

_____

_____

_____

_____

_____

_____

DRAWINGS

I ACCOMPLISHED	DATE	THINGS TO DO
1. _____		• _____
2. _____		• _____
3. _____		• _____
4. _____		• _____
5. _____		• _____

134

GOALS	I NEED
○ _____	☐ _____
○ _____	☐ _____
○ _____	☐ _____
○ _____	☐ _____
○ _____	☐ _____
○ _____	☐ _____

MY NOTES

MONDAY:

MY INVENTION IS: _____

_____

_____

_____

_____

_____

_____

_____

_____

_____

DRAWINGS

I ACCOMPLISHED	DATE	THINGS TO DO
1. _____		• _____
2. _____		• _____
3. _____		• _____
4. _____		• _____
5. _____		• _____

GOALS

- ○ _____
- ○ _____
- ○ _____
- ○ _____
- ○ _____
- ○ _____

I NEED

- ☐ _____
- ☐ _____
- ☐ _____
- ☐ _____
- ☐ _____
- ☐ _____

MY NOTES

TUESDAY:

MY INVENTION IS: _____

_____

_____

_____

_____

NOTES

_____

_____

_____

_____

_____

DRAWINGS

I ACCOMPLISHED	DATE	THINGS TO DO
1. _____		• _____
2. _____		• _____
3. _____		• _____
4. _____		• _____
5. _____		• _____

GOALS

- _____
- _____
- _____
- _____
- _____
- _____

I NEED

- [ ] _____
- [ ] _____
- [ ] _____
- [ ] _____
- [ ] _____
- [ ] _____

MY NOTES

WEDNESDAY:

MY INVENTION IS: _____

_____

_____

_____

_____

_____

_____

_____

_____

_____

DRAWINGS

I ACCOMPLISHED	DATE	THINGS TO DO
1. _____		• _____
2. _____		• _____
3. _____		• _____
4. _____		• _____
5. _____		• _____

140

GOALS

I NEED

- ○ _____
- ○ _____
- ○ _____
- ○ _____
- ○ _____
- ○ _____

- ☐ _____
- ☐ _____
- ☐ _____
- ☐ _____
- ☐ _____
- ☐ _____

MY NOTES

THURSDAY:

MY INVENTION IS: _____

_____

_____

_____

_____

_____

_____

_____

_____

DRAWINGS

I ACCOMPLISHED	DATE	THINGS TO DO
1. _____		• _____
2. _____		• _____
3. _____		• _____
4. _____		• _____
5. _____		• _____

GOALS

- ○ _____
- ○ _____
- ○ _____
- ○ _____
- ○ _____
- ○ _____

I NEED

- ☐ _____
- ☐ _____
- ☐ _____
- ☐ _____
- ☐ _____
- ☐ _____

MY NOTES

FRIDAY:

MY INVENTION IS: _____

_____

_____

_____

_____

_____

_____

_____

_____

_____

DRAWINGS

I ACCOMPLISHED	DATE	THINGS TO DO
1. _____		• _____
2. _____		• _____
3. _____		• _____
4. _____		• _____
5. _____		• _____

GOALS

- ○ _____
- ○ _____
- ○ _____
- ○ _____
- ○ _____
- ○ _____

I NEED

- ☐ _____
- ☐ _____
- ☐ _____
- ☐ _____
- ☐ _____
- ☐ _____

MY NOTES

SATURDAY:

MY INVENTION IS: _____
_____
_____
_____
_____

NOTES
_____
_____
_____
_____
_____

DRAWINGS

I ACCOMPLISHED	DATE	THINGS TO DO
1. _____		• _____
2. _____		• _____
3. _____		• _____
4. _____		• _____
5. _____		• _____

GOALS

- ○ _____
- ○ _____
- ○ _____
- ○ _____
- ○ _____
- ○ _____

I NEED

- ☐ _____
- ☐ _____
- ☐ _____
- ☐ _____
- ☐ _____
- ☐ _____

MY NOTES

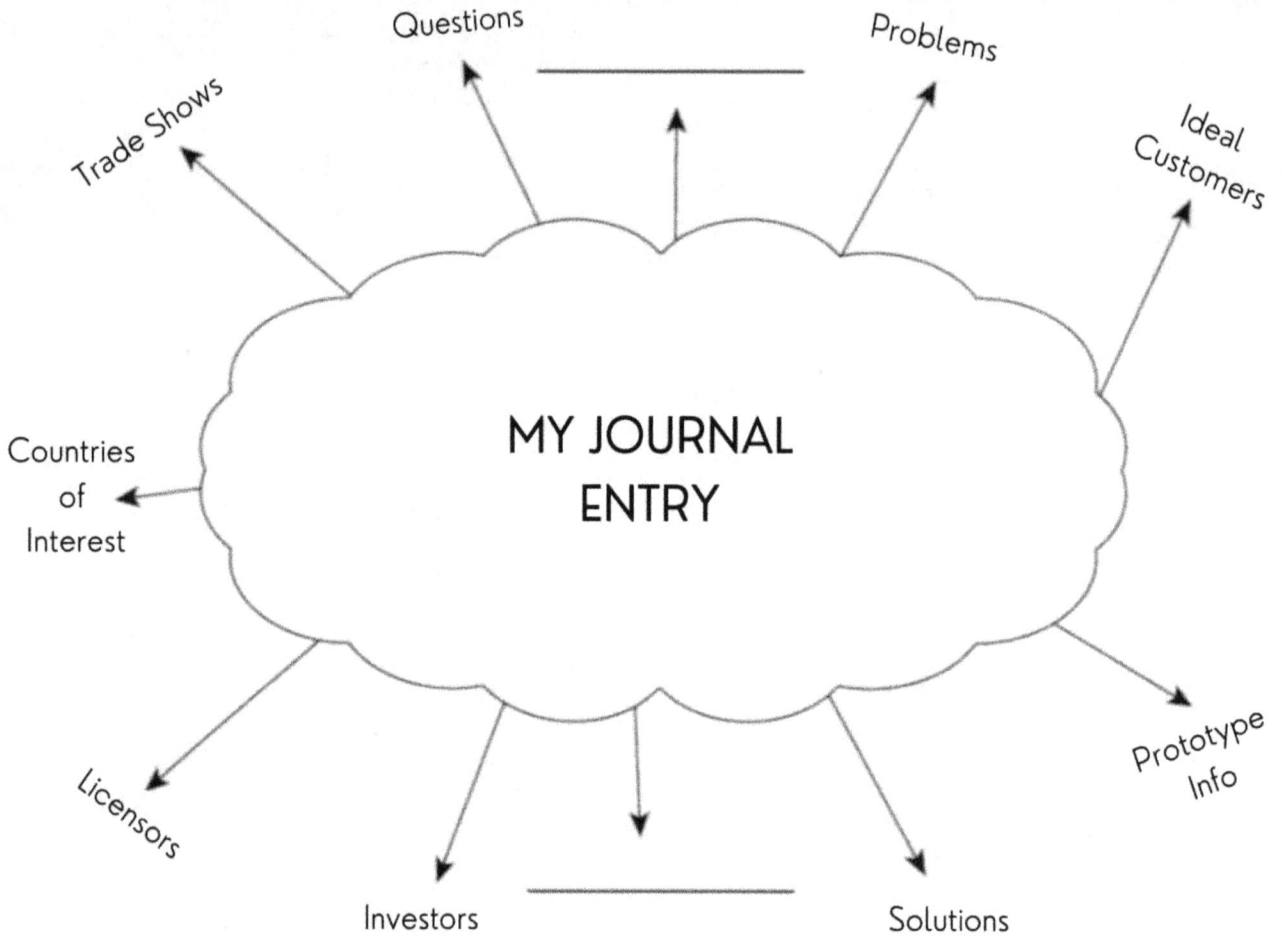

Questions

Problems

Trade Shows

Ideal Customers

Countries of Interest

MY JOURNAL ENTRY

Licensors

Prototype Info

Investors

Solutions

_____

_____

_____

_____

_____

_____

_____

MY JOURNAL ENTRY FOR THE WEEK OF:

_____

_____

_____

_____

_____

_____

_____

_____

_____

_____

_____

_____

_____

_____

_____

_____

_____

_____

MY JOURNAL ENTRY FOR THE WEEK OF:

RESOURCES

REFERENCES

IMPORTANT INFORMATION ABOUT MY INVENTION

IMPORTANT DATES

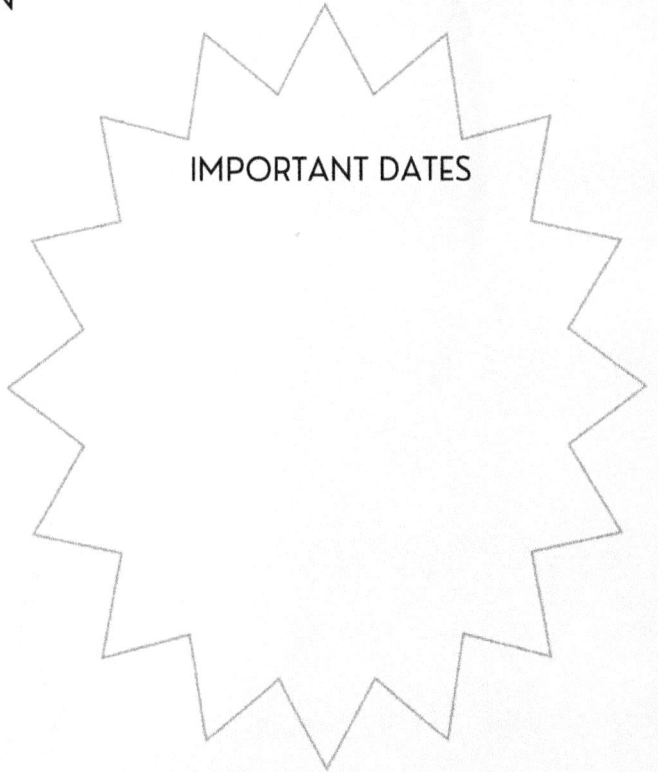

I SPOKE TO

-
-
-
-
-
-

MISC.

I FEEL

happy

sad

worried

angry

SUNDAY:

MY INVENTION IS: _____

_____

_____

_____

_____

NOTES

_____

_____

_____

_____

_____

_____

DRAWINGS

I ACCOMPLISHED	DATE	THINGS TO DO
1. _____		• _____
2. _____		• _____
3. _____		• _____
4. _____		• _____
5. _____		• _____

GOALS

I NEED

MY NOTES

MONDAY:

MY INVENTION IS: _____

_____

_____

_____

_____

_____

_____

_____

_____

DRAWINGS

I ACCOMPLISHED	DATE	THINGS TO DO
1. _____		• _____
2. _____		• _____
3. _____		• _____
4. _____		• _____
5. _____		• _____

GOALS

- ○ _____
- ○ _____
- ○ _____
- ○ _____
- ○ _____
- ○ _____

I NEED

- ☐ _____
- ☐ _____
- ☐ _____
- ☐ _____
- ☐ _____
- ☐ _____

MY NOTES

_____
_____
_____
_____
_____
_____
_____
_____
_____
_____
_____
_____
_____
_____
_____
_____
_____
_____
_____
_____

TUESDAY:

MY INVENTION IS: _____

_____

_____

_____

_____

NOTES

_____

_____

_____

_____

_____

DRAWINGS

I ACCOMPLISHED	DATE	THINGS TO DO
1. _____		• _____
2. _____		• _____
3. _____		• _____
4. _____		• _____
5. _____		• _____

GOALS

I NEED

○ _____

○ _____

○ _____

○ _____

○ _____

○ _____

☐ _____

☐ _____

☐ _____

☐ _____

☐ _____

☐ _____

MY NOTES

WEDNESDAY:

MY INVENTION IS: _____
_____
_____
_____
_____

NOTES
_____
_____
_____
_____
_____

DRAWINGS

I ACCOMPLISHED	DATE	THINGS TO DO
1. _____		• _____
2. _____		• _____
3. _____		• _____
4. _____		• _____
5. _____		• _____

GOALS

- ○ _____
- ○ _____
- ○ _____
- ○ _____
- ○ _____
- ○ _____

I NEED

- ☐ _____
- ☐ _____
- ☐ _____
- ☐ _____
- ☐ _____
- ☐ _____

MY NOTES

THURSDAY:

MY INVENTION IS: _____

_____

_____

_____

_____

_____

_____

_____

_____

_____

DRAWINGS

I ACCOMPLISHED	DATE	THINGS TO DO
1. _____		• _____
2. _____		• _____
3. _____		• _____
4. _____		• _____
5. _____		• _____

GOALS

-
-
-
-
-
-

I NEED

- [ ]
- [ ]
- [ ]
- [ ]
- [ ]
- [ ]

MY NOTES

FRIDAY:

MY INVENTION IS:

_____

_____
_____
_____
_____

NOTES

_____
_____
_____
_____
_____

DRAWINGS

I ACCOMPLISHED	DATE	THINGS TO DO
1. _____		• _____
2. _____		• _____
3. _____		• _____
4. _____		• _____
5. _____		• _____

GOALS

- ○ _____
- ○ _____
- ○ _____
- ○ _____
- ○ _____
- ○ _____

I NEED

- ☐ _____
- ☐ _____
- ☐ _____
- ☐ _____
- ☐ _____
- ☐ _____

MY NOTES

SATURDAY:

MY INVENTION IS: _____

_____
_____
_____
_____

_____
_____
_____
_____
_____

DRAWINGS

I ACCOMPLISHED	DATE	THINGS TO DO
1. _____		• _____
2. _____		• _____
3. _____		• _____
4. _____		• _____
5. _____		• _____

GOALS

- ○ _____
- ○ _____
- ○ _____
- ○ _____
- ○ _____
- ○ _____

I NEED

- ☐ _____
- ☐ _____
- ☐ _____
- ☐ _____
- ☐ _____
- ☐ _____

MY NOTES

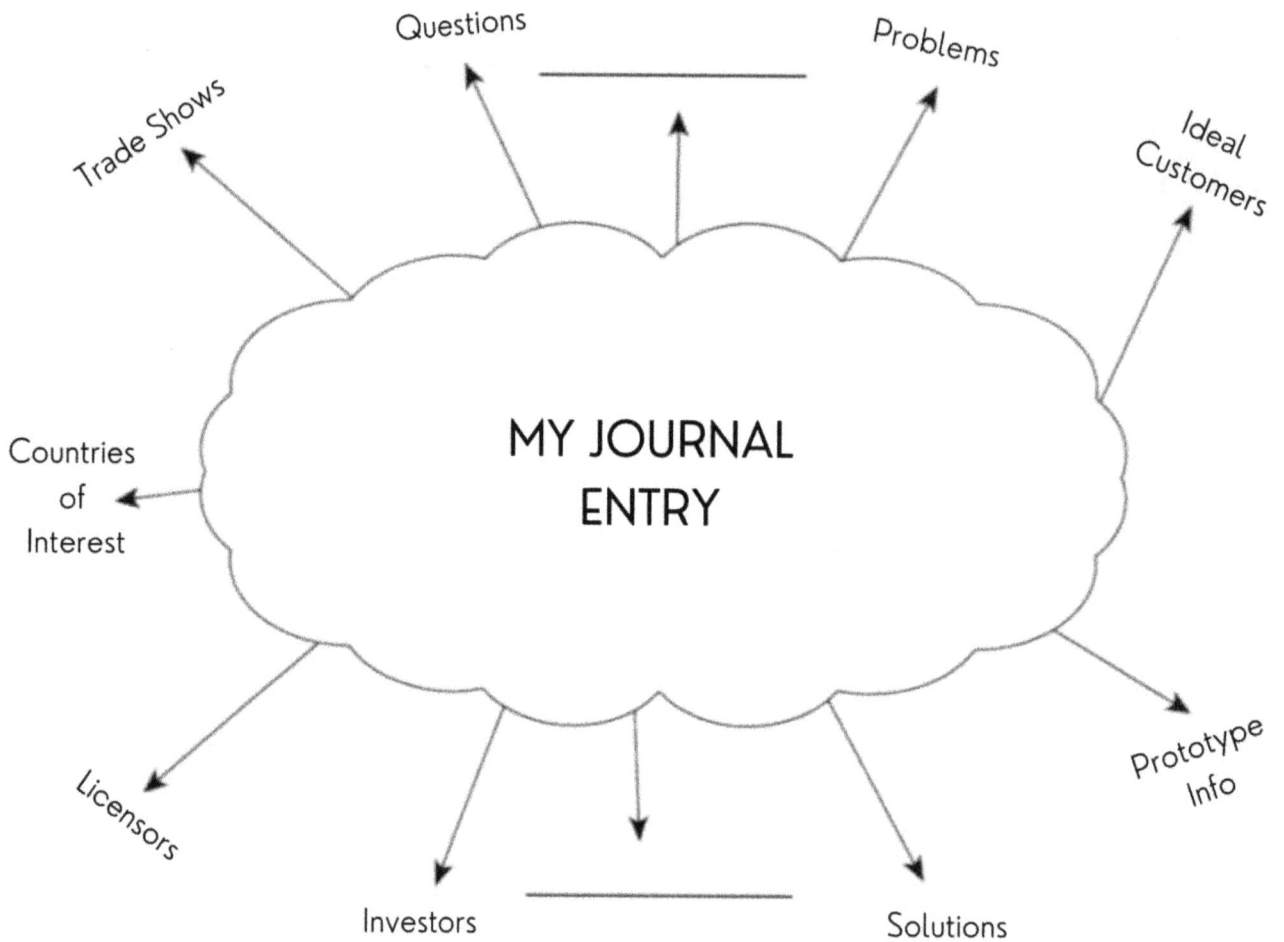

Questions

Problems

Trade Shows

Ideal Customers

Countries of Interest

MY JOURNAL ENTRY

Licensors

Prototype Info

Investors

Solutions

MY JOURNAL ENTRY FOR THE WEEK OF:

_____

_____

_____

_____

_____

_____

_____

_____

_____

_____

_____

_____

_____

_____

_____

_____

_____

_____

MY JOURNAL ENTRY FOR THE WEEK OF:

RESOURCES	REFERENCES

IMPORTANT INFORMATION ABOUT MY INVENTION

IMPORTANT DATES

I SPOKE TO	MISC.	I FEEL
•		happy sad
•		
•		
•		worried angry
•		
•		

MARCH

IT'S TIME TO
WORK!

MARCH:

SUNDAY	MONDAY	TUESDAY	WEDNESDAY

THURSDAY	FRIDAY	SATURDAY	IMPORTANT
			☐
			☐
			☐
			☐
			☐
			☐
			☐
			☐
			☐
			☐
			☐
			☐
			☐

NOTES

SUNDAY:

MY INVENTION IS: _____

_____
_____
_____
_____

NOTES

_____
_____
_____
_____
_____

DRAWINGS

I ACCOMPLISHED	DATE	THINGS TO DO
1. _____		• _____
2. _____		• _____
3. _____		• _____
4. _____		• _____
5. _____		• _____

GOALS

- ○ _____
- ○ _____
- ○ _____
- ○ _____
- ○ _____
- ○ _____

I NEED

- ☐ _____
- ☐ _____
- ☐ _____
- ☐ _____
- ☐ _____
- ☐ _____

MY NOTES

MONDAY:

MY INVENTION IS: _____

_____

_____

_____

_____

_____

_____

_____

_____

_____

DRAWINGS

I ACCOMPLISHED	DATE	THINGS TO DO
1. _____		• _____
2. _____		• _____
3. _____		• _____
4. _____		• _____
5. _____		• _____

GOALS

I NEED

- ○ _____
- ○ _____
- ○ _____
- ○ _____
- ○ _____
- ○ _____

- ☐ _____
- ☐ _____
- ☐ _____
- ☐ _____
- ☐ _____
- ☐ _____

MY NOTES

TUESDAY:

MY INVENTION IS: _____

_____

_____

_____

NOTES

_____

_____

_____

_____

_____

DRAWINGS

I ACCOMPLISHED	DATE	THINGS TO DO
1. _____		• _____
2. _____		• _____
3. _____		• _____
4. _____		• _____
5. _____		• _____

GOALS

- ○ _____
- ○ _____
- ○ _____
- ○ _____
- ○ _____
- ○ _____

I NEED

- ☐ _____
- ☐ _____
- ☐ _____
- ☐ _____
- ☐ _____
- ☐ _____

MY NOTES

WEDNESDAY:

MY INVENTION IS: _____

_____

_____

_____

_____

_____

_____

_____

_____

_____

DRAWINGS

I ACCOMPLISHED	DATE	THINGS TO DO
1. _____		• _____
2. _____		• _____
3. _____		• _____
4. _____		• _____
5. _____		• _____

GOALS

- ○ _____
- ○ _____
- ○ _____
- ○ _____
- ○ _____
- ○ _____

I NEED

- ☐ _____
- ☐ _____
- ☐ _____
- ☐ _____
- ☐ _____
- ☐ _____

MY NOTES

THURSDAY:

MY INVENTION IS: _____

_____

_____

_____

_____

NOTES

_____

_____

_____

_____

DRAWINGS

I ACCOMPLISHED	DATE	THINGS TO DO
1. _____		• _____
2. _____		• _____
3. _____		• _____
4. _____		• _____
5. _____		• _____

GOALS

- ○ _____
- ○ _____
- ○ _____
- ○ _____
- ○ _____
- ○ _____

I NEED

- ☐ _____
- ☐ _____
- ☐ _____
- ☐ _____
- ☐ _____
- ☐ _____

MY NOTES

FRIDAY:

MY INVENTION IS: _____
_____
_____
_____
_____

NOTES
_____
_____
_____
_____
_____

DRAWINGS

I ACCOMPLISHED	DATE	THINGS TO DO
1. _____		• _____
2. _____		• _____
3. _____		• _____
4. _____		• _____
5. _____		• _____

GOALS

- _____
- _____
- _____
- _____
- _____
- _____

I NEED

- [ ] _____
- [ ] _____
- [ ] _____
- [ ] _____
- [ ] _____
- [ ] _____

MY NOTES

SATURDAY:

MY INVENTION IS:

_____

_____

_____

_____

NOTES

_____

_____

_____

_____

_____

DRAWINGS

I ACCOMPLISHED	DATE	THINGS TO DO
1. _____		• _____
2. _____		• _____
3. _____		• _____
4. _____		• _____
5. _____		• _____

GOALS

- ○ _____
- ○ _____
- ○ _____
- ○ _____
- ○ _____
- ○ _____

I NEED

- ☐ _____
- ☐ _____
- ☐ _____
- ☐ _____
- ☐ _____
- ☐ _____

MY NOTES

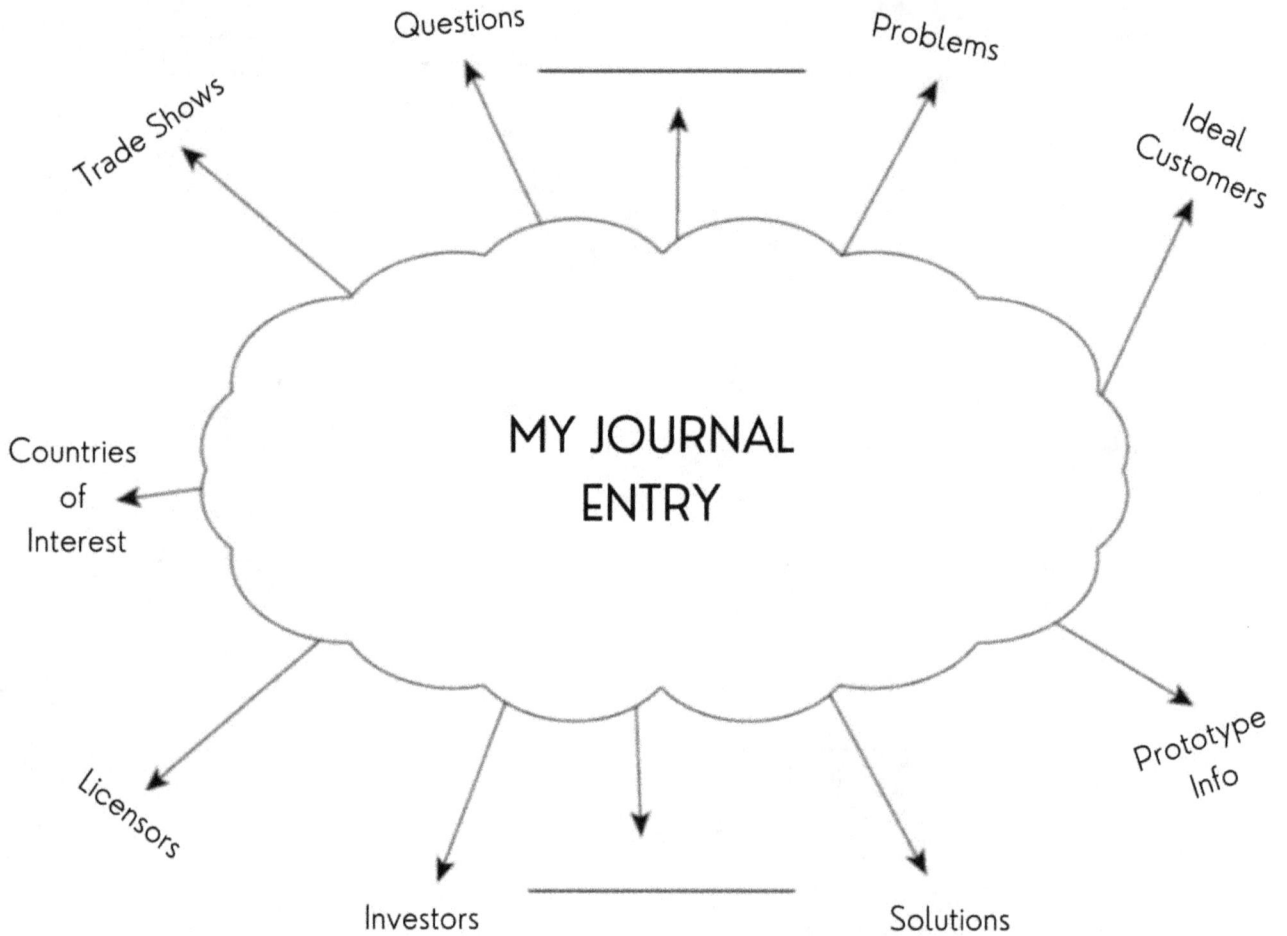

Questions

Problems

Trade Shows

Ideal Customers

MY JOURNAL ENTRY

Countries of Interest

Licensors

Prototype Info

Investors

Solutions

MY JOURNAL ENTRY FOR THE WEEK OF:

_____

_____

_____

_____

_____

_____

_____

_____

_____

_____

_____

_____

_____

_____

_____

_____

_____

_____

IMPORTANT INFORMATION ABOUT MY INVENTION

IMPORTANT DATES

I SPOKE TO

MISC.

I FEEL

happy

sad

worried

angry

SUNDAY:

MY INVENTION IS: _____
_____
_____
_____
_____

_____
_____
_____
_____
_____

DRAWINGS

I ACCOMPLISHED	DATE	THINGS TO DO
1. _____		• _____
2. _____		• _____
3. _____		• _____
4. _____		• _____
5. _____		• _____

GOALS	I NEED
○ _____	☐ _____
○ _____	☐ _____
○ _____	☐ _____
○ _____	☐ _____
○ _____	☐ _____
○ _____	☐ _____

MY NOTES

MONDAY:

MY INVENTION IS: _____

_____

_____

_____

_____

_____

_____

_____

_____

DRAWINGS

I ACCOMPLISHED	DATE	THINGS TO DO
1. _____		• _____
2. _____		• _____
3. _____		• _____
4. _____		• _____
5. _____		• _____

GOALS

- ○ _____
- ○ _____
- ○ _____
- ○ _____
- ○ _____
- ○ _____

I NEED

- ☐ _____
- ☐ _____
- ☐ _____
- ☐ _____
- ☐ _____
- ☐ _____

MY NOTES

TUESDAY:

MY INVENTION IS: _____

_____

_____

_____

_____

NOTES

_____

_____

_____

_____

_____

DRAWINGS

I ACCOMPLISHED	DATE	THINGS TO DO
1. _____		• _____
2. _____		• _____
3. _____		• _____
4. _____		• _____
5. _____		• _____

GOALS

- ○ _____
- ○ _____
- ○ _____
- ○ _____
- ○ _____
- ○ _____

I NEED

- ☐ _____
- ☐ _____
- ☐ _____
- ☐ _____
- ☐ _____
- ☐ _____

MY NOTES

WEDNESDAY:

MY INVENTION IS: _____

_____
_____
_____
_____

_____
_____
_____
_____
_____

DRAWINGS

I ACCOMPLISHED	DATE	THINGS TO DO
1. _____		• _____
2. _____		• _____
3. _____		• _____
4. _____		• _____
5. _____		• _____

GOALS

- _____
- _____
- _____
- _____
- _____
- _____

I NEED

- [ ] _____
- [ ] _____
- [ ] _____
- [ ] _____
- [ ] _____
- [ ] _____

MY NOTES

_____
_____
_____
_____
_____
_____
_____
_____
_____
_____
_____
_____
_____
_____
_____
_____
_____

THURSDAY:

MY INVENTION IS: _____

_____

_____

_____

_____

_____

_____

_____

_____

_____

DRAWINGS

I ACCOMPLISHED	DATE	THINGS TO DO
1. _____		• _____
2. _____		• _____
3. _____		• _____
4. _____		• _____
5. _____		• _____

GOALS

- ○ _____
- ○ _____
- ○ _____
- ○ _____
- ○ _____
- ○ _____

I NEED

- ☐ _____
- ☐ _____
- ☐ _____
- ☐ _____
- ☐ _____
- ☐ _____

MY NOTES

FRIDAY:

MY INVENTION IS: _____

_____

_____

_____

_____

_____

_____

_____

_____

_____

DRAWINGS

I ACCOMPLISHED	DATE	THINGS TO DO
1. _____		• _____
2. _____		• _____
3. _____		• _____
4. _____		• _____
5. _____		• _____

GOALS

I NEED

MY NOTES

SATURDAY:

MY INVENTION IS: _____
_____
_____
_____
_____

NOTES
_____
_____
_____
_____
_____

DRAWINGS

I ACCOMPLISHED	DATE	THINGS TO DO
1. _____		• _____
2. _____		• _____
3. _____		• _____
4. _____		• _____
5. _____		• _____

GOALS	I NEED
○ _____	☐ _____
○ _____	☐ _____
○ _____	☐ _____
○ _____	☐ _____
○ _____	☐ _____
○ _____	☐ _____

MY NOTES

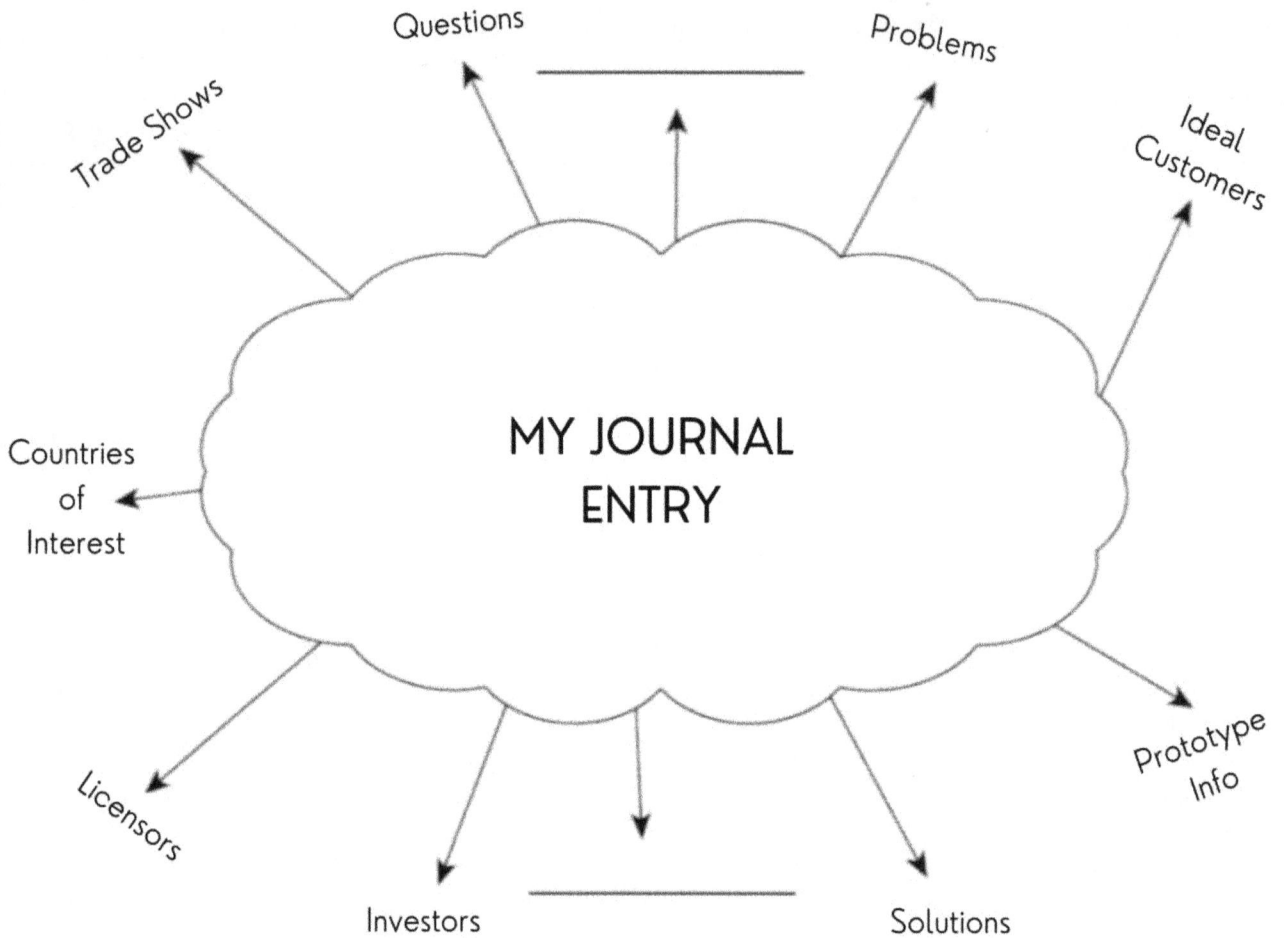

Questions

Problems

Trade Shows

Ideal Customers

Countries of Interest

MY JOURNAL ENTRY

Licensors

Prototype Info

Investors

Solutions

MY JOURNAL ENTRY FOR THE WEEK OF:

_____

_____

_____

_____

_____

_____

_____

_____

_____

_____

_____

_____

_____

_____

_____

_____

_____

_____

MY JOURNAL ENTRY FOR THE WEEK OF:

RESOURCES

REFERENCES

IMPORTANT INFORMATION ABOUT MY INVENTION

IMPORTANT DATES

I SPOKE TO

-
-
-
-
-
-

MISC.

I FEEL

happy

sad

worried

angry

SUNDAY:

MY INVENTION IS: _____
_____
_____
_____
_____

NOTES
_____
_____
_____
_____
_____

DRAWINGS

I ACCOMPLISHED	DATE	THINGS TO DO
1. _____		• _____
2. _____		• _____
3. _____		• _____
4. _____		• _____
5. _____		• _____

GOALS

- ○ _____
- ○ _____
- ○ _____
- ○ _____
- ○ _____
- ○ _____

I NEED

- ☐ _____
- ☐ _____
- ☐ _____
- ☐ _____
- ☐ _____
- ☐ _____

MY NOTES

_____

_____

_____

_____

_____

_____

_____

_____

_____

_____

_____

_____

_____

_____

_____

_____

_____

_____

_____

MONDAY:

MY INVENTION IS: _____

_____

_____

_____

_____

_____

_____

_____

_____

_____

DRAWINGS

I ACCOMPLISHED	DATE	THINGS TO DO
1. _____		• _____
2. _____		• _____
3. _____		• _____
4. _____		• _____
5. _____		• _____

GOALS

- ○ _____
- ○ _____
- ○ _____
- ○ _____
- ○ _____
- ○ _____

I NEED

- ☐ _____
- ☐ _____
- ☐ _____
- ☐ _____
- ☐ _____
- ☐ _____

MY NOTES

TUESDAY:

MY INVENTION IS: _____

_____
_____
_____
_____

_____
_____
_____
_____
_____

DRAWINGS

I ACCOMPLISHED	DATE	THINGS TO DO
1. _____		• _____
2. _____		• _____
3. _____		• _____
4. _____		• _____
5. _____		• _____

GOALS

- _____
- _____
- _____
- _____
- _____
- _____

I NEED

- ☐ _____
- ☐ _____
- ☐ _____
- ☐ _____
- ☐ _____
- ☐ _____

MY NOTES

_____

_____

_____

_____

_____

_____

_____

_____

_____

_____

_____

_____

_____

_____

_____

_____

WEDNESDAY:

MY INVENTION IS: _____

_____
_____
_____
_____

_____
_____
_____
_____
_____

DRAWINGS

I ACCOMPLISHED	DATE	THINGS TO DO
1. _____		• _____
2. _____		• _____
3. _____		• _____
4. _____		• _____
5. _____		• _____

GOALS

- ○ _____
- ○ _____
- ○ _____
- ○ _____
- ○ _____
- ○ _____

I NEED

- ☐ _____
- ☐ _____
- ☐ _____
- ☐ _____
- ☐ _____
- ☐ _____

MY NOTES

THURSDAY:

MY INVENTION IS: _____

_____

_____

_____

_____

_____

_____

_____

_____

_____

DRAWINGS

I ACCOMPLISHED	DATE	THINGS TO DO
1. _____		• _____
2. _____		• _____
3. _____		• _____
4. _____		• _____
5. _____		• _____

218

GOALS

- _____
- _____
- _____
- _____
- _____
- _____

I NEED

- [ ] _____
- [ ] _____
- [ ] _____
- [ ] _____
- [ ] _____
- [ ] _____

MY NOTES

FRIDAY:

MY INVENTION IS: _____
_____
_____
_____
_____

_____
_____
_____
_____
_____

DRAWINGS

I ACCOMPLISHED	DATE	THINGS TO DO
1. _____	_____	• _____
2. _____	_____	• _____
3. _____	_____	• _____
4. _____	_____	• _____
5. _____	_____	• _____

GOALS

- ○ _____
- ○ _____
- ○ _____
- ○ _____
- ○ _____
- ○ _____

I NEED

- ☐ _____
- ☐ _____
- ☐ _____
- ☐ _____
- ☐ _____
- ☐ _____

MY NOTES

_____
_____
_____
_____
_____
_____
_____
_____
_____
_____
_____
_____
_____
_____
_____
_____
_____
_____
_____

SATURDAY:

MY INVENTION IS: _____

_____

_____

_____

_____

_____

_____

_____

_____

_____

DRAWINGS

I ACCOMPLISHED	DATE	THINGS TO DO
1. _____		• _____
2. _____		• _____
3. _____		• _____
4. _____		• _____
5. _____		• _____

GOALS	I NEED
○ _____	☐ _____
○ _____	☐ _____
○ _____	☐ _____
○ _____	☐ _____
○ _____	☐ _____
○ _____	☐ _____

MY NOTES

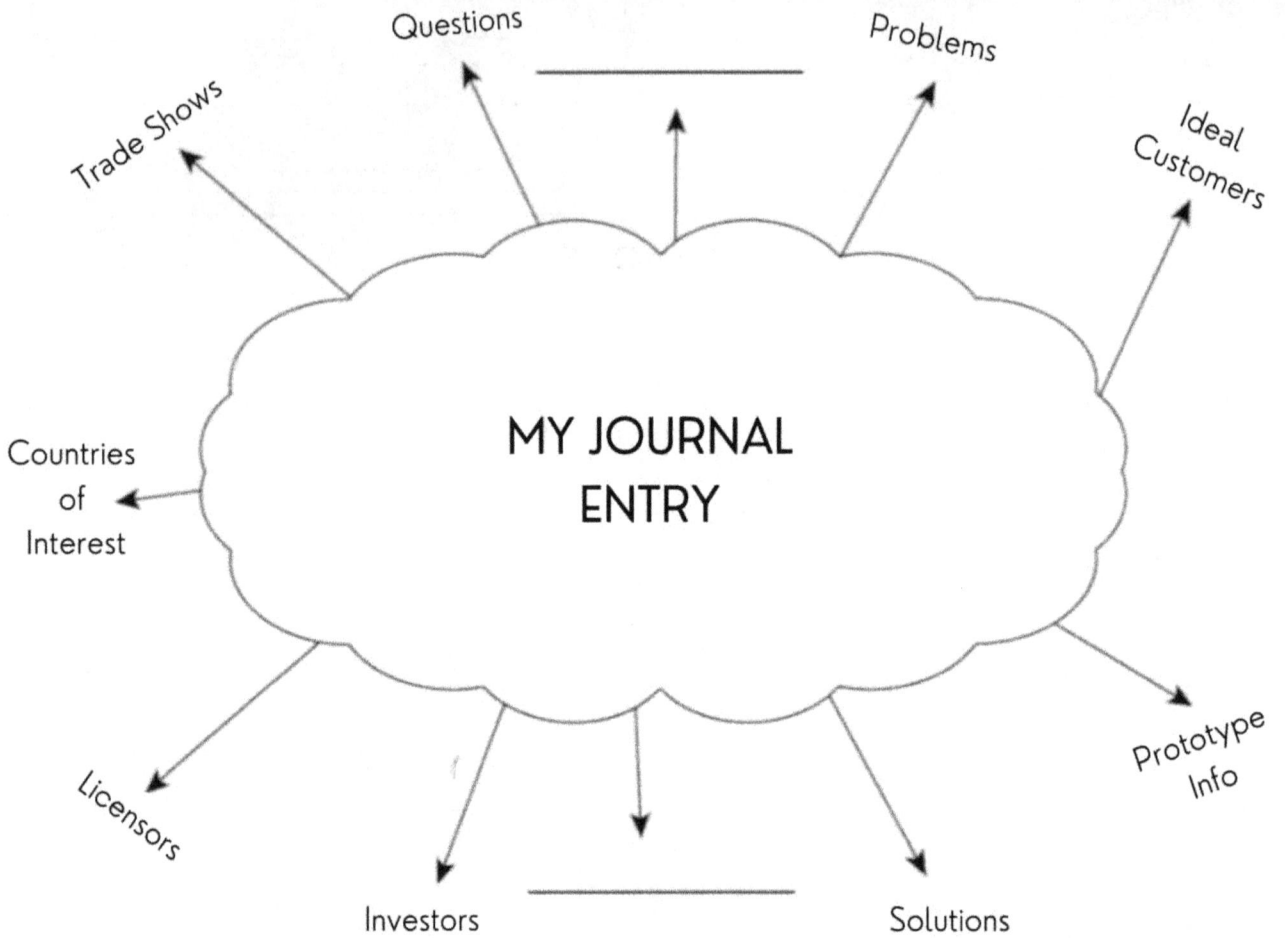

Questions _____ Problems

Trade Shows

Ideal Customers

Countries of Interest

MY JOURNAL ENTRY

Licensors

Prototype Info

Investors _____ Solutions

_____

_____

_____

_____

_____

_____

_____

MY JOURNAL ENTRY FOR THE WEEK OF:

_____

_____

_____

_____

_____

_____

_____

_____

_____

_____

_____

_____

_____

_____

_____

_____

_____

_____

MY JOURNAL ENTRY FOR THE WEEK OF:

_____

_____

_____

_____

_____

_____

_____

_____

_____

_____

_____

_____

_____

_____

_____

_____

_____

_____

_____

_____

RESOURCES

REFERENCES

IMPORTANT INFORMATION ABOUT MY INVENTION

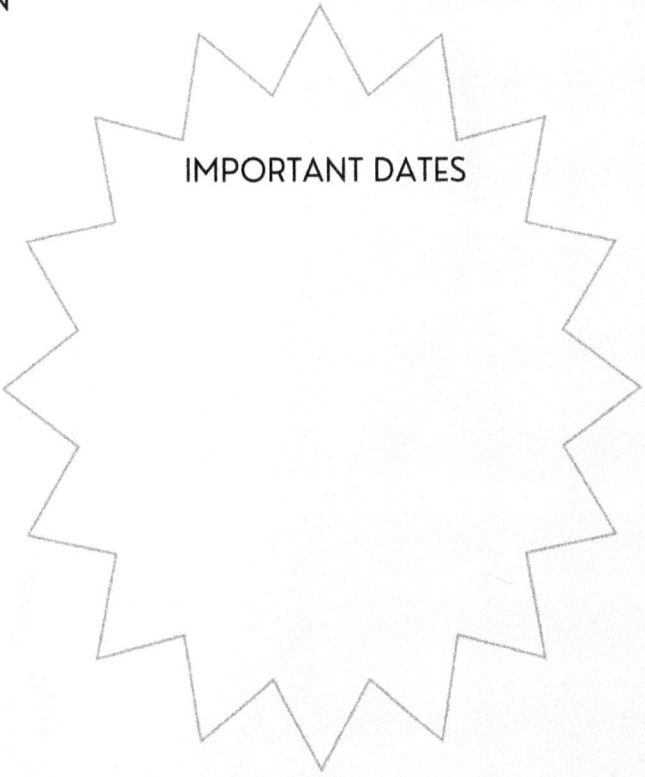

IMPORTANT DATES

I SPOKE TO

-
-
-
-
-
-

MISC.

I FEEL

happy

sad

worried

angry

MY INVENTION IS:

_____

_____

_____

_____

NOTES

_____

_____

_____

_____

_____

DRAWINGS

I ACCOMPLISHED	DATE	THINGS TO DO
1. _____		• _____
2. _____		• _____
3. _____		• _____
4. _____		• _____
5. _____		• _____

GOALS

- ○ _____
- ○ _____
- ○ _____
- ○ _____
- ○ _____
- ○ _____

I NEED

- ☐ _____
- ☐ _____
- ☐ _____
- ☐ _____
- ☐ _____
- ☐ _____

MY NOTES

MONDAY:

MY INVENTION IS: _____

_____

_____

_____

_____

_____

_____

_____

_____

_____

DRAWINGS

I ACCOMPLISHED	DATE	THINGS TO DO
1. _____		• _____
2. _____		• _____
3. _____		• _____
4. _____		• _____
5. _____		• _____

GOALS

- ○ _____
- ○ _____
- ○ _____
- ○ _____
- ○ _____
- ○ _____

I NEED

- ☐ _____
- ☐ _____
- ☐ _____
- ☐ _____
- ☐ _____
- ☐ _____

MY NOTES

TUESDAY:

MY INVENTION IS: _____
_____
_____
_____
_____

_____
_____
_____
_____
_____

DRAWINGS

I ACCOMPLISHED	DATE	THINGS TO DO
1. _____		• _____
2. _____		• _____
3. _____		• _____
4. _____		• _____
5. _____		• _____

GOALS

I NEED

MY NOTES

WEDNESDAY:

MY INVENTION IS: _____

_____

_____

_____

_____

_____

_____

_____

_____

DRAWINGS

I ACCOMPLISHED	DATE	THINGS TO DO
1. _____		• _____
2. _____		• _____
3. _____		• _____
4. _____		• _____
5. _____		• _____

234

GOALS

- ○ _____
- ○ _____
- ○ _____
- ○ _____
- ○ _____
- ○ _____

I NEED

- ☐ _____
- ☐ _____
- ☐ _____
- ☐ _____
- ☐ _____
- ☐ _____

MY NOTES

THURSDAY:

MY INVENTION IS: _____

_____
_____
_____
_____

_____
_____
_____
_____
_____

DRAWINGS

I ACCOMPLISHED	DATE	THINGS TO DO
1. _____		• _____
2. _____		• _____
3. _____		• _____
4. _____		• _____
5. _____		• _____

GOALS

- ○ _____
- ○ _____
- ○ _____
- ○ _____
- ○ _____
- ○ _____

I NEED

- ☐ _____
- ☐ _____
- ☐ _____
- ☐ _____
- ☐ _____
- ☐ _____

MY NOTES

_____

_____

_____

_____

_____

_____

_____

_____

_____

_____

_____

_____

_____

_____

_____

_____

_____

_____

_____

FRIDAY:

MY INVENTION IS: _____
_____
_____
_____
_____

_____
_____
_____
_____
_____

DRAWINGS

I ACCOMPLISHED	DATE	THINGS TO DO
1. _____		• _____
2. _____		• _____
3. _____		• _____
4. _____		• _____
5. _____		• _____

GOALS

- ○ _____
- ○ _____
- ○ _____
- ○ _____
- ○ _____
- ○ _____

I NEED

- ☐ _____
- ☐ _____
- ☐ _____
- ☐ _____
- ☐ _____
- ☐ _____

MY NOTES

SATURDAY:

MY INVENTION IS: _____

_____

_____

_____

_____

NOTES

_____

_____

_____

_____

_____

DRAWINGS

I ACCOMPLISHED	DATE	THINGS TO DO
1. _____		• _____
2. _____		• _____
3. _____		• _____
4. _____		• _____
5. _____		• _____

GOALS

- ○ _____
- ○ _____
- ○ _____
- ○ _____
- ○ _____
- ○ _____

I NEED

- ☐ _____
- ☐ _____
- ☐ _____
- ☐ _____
- ☐ _____
- ☐ _____

MY NOTES

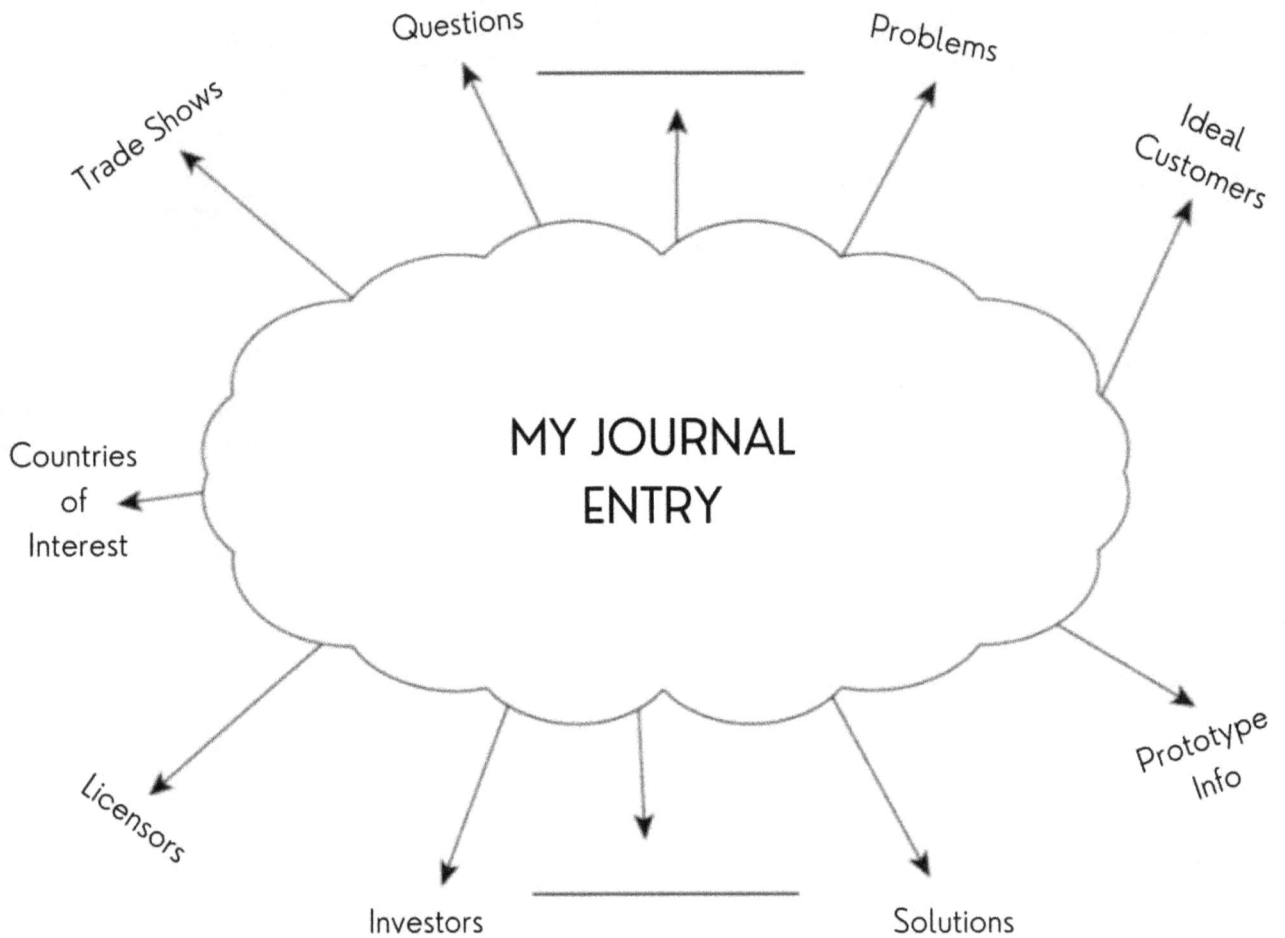

Questions

Problems

Trade Shows

Ideal Customers

MY JOURNAL ENTRY

Countries of Interest

Licensors

Prototype Info

Investors

Solutions

MY JOURNAL ENTRY FOR THE WEEK OF:

_____

_____

_____

_____

_____

_____

_____

_____

_____

_____

_____

_____

_____

_____

_____

_____

_____

_____

MY JOURNAL ENTRY FOR THE WEEK OF:

RESOURCES	REFERENCES

IMPORTANT INFORMATION ABOUT MY INVENTION

IMPORTANT DATES

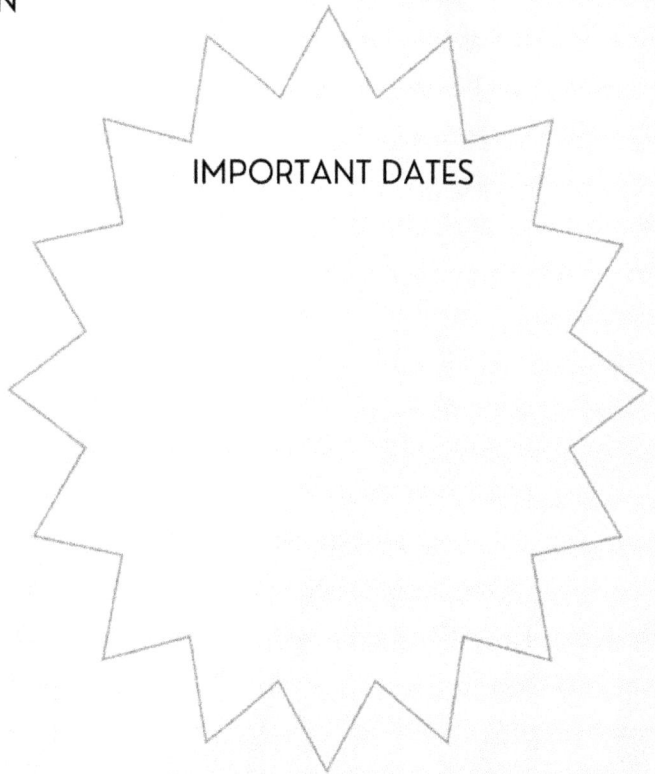

I SPOKE TO	MISC.	I FEEL
•		happy
•		sad
•		worried
•		angry
•		
•		

ABOUT THE AUTHOR

Andrea Hence Evans, Esq. is the owner of The Law Firm of Andrea Hence Evans, LLC. Her career path is unique since she worked at the United States Patent and Trademark Office (USPTO) for approximately 5 years as both a Patent Examiner and a Trademark Examining Attorney after graduating from law school.

Andrea Hence Evans, Esq. is a graduate of The George Washington Law School in Washington, DC. While attending law school, she took advantage of the school's world renowned intellectual property curriculum. She is a graduate of Spelman College and Georgia Institute of Technology (Georgia Tech) in Atlanta, Georgia, where she obtained a Bachelors of Science in Mathematics and a Bachelors of Civil and Environmental Engineering, respectively.

Andrea Hence Evans, Esq. is a member of the Texas bar. She is also a registered Patent Attorney. She is a member of the US Supreme Court Bar. She has won numerous awards and she is a frequent speaker about intellectual property at conferences around the world. She has been featured on NBC, ABC, CBS and PBS, to name a few. The Firm currently represents clients globally with US intellectual property matters.

Andrea is a Patent Attorney on the television show, Make48. She is a wife, mother of two, and owner of KidGINEER, LLC, a hands-on science, technology, engineering and math (STEM) program.

She is an award-winning and best selling author of All About Inventing: Everything You Need to Know About Patents From a Former USPTO Patent Examiner & Patent Attorney and the book, All About Trademarks: Everything You Need to Know About Trademarks From a Former USPTO Trademark Examining Attorney.

Twitter: www.twitter.com/evansiplaw
FB: www.facebook.com/evansiplaw
Instagram: www.instagram.com/evansiplaw
Website: www.evansiplaw.com
Email: info@evansiplaw.com
(301) 497-9997